POOI
Private Pilot's Guide

JAR

Aviation Law
& Operational Procedures

David Cockburn

Nothing in this syllabus supersedes any legislation, rules, regulations or procedures contained in any operational document issued by Her Majesty's Stationery Office, the Civil Aviation Authority, the Joint Aviation Authorities, ICAO, the manufacturers of aircraft, engines and systems, or by the operators of aircraft throughout the world.

JAR Aviation Law & Operational Procedures

© David Cockburn 2004

ISBN 1-84336-056-X

Air Pilot Publishing Ltd
Mill Road • Cranfield • Bedfordshire • MK43 0JG • England
Telephone: 01234 750677 • Facsimile: 01234 750706
Email: sales@appltd.net • Website: www.pooleys.com

All rights reserved. No part of this publication may be reproduced in any material form (including photocopying or storing it in any medium by electronic means and whether or not transiently or incidentally to some of the use of this publication (without the written permission of the copyright owner) except in accordance with the provisions of the Copyright, Designs and Patents Act 1988 or under the terms of a licence issued by the Copyright Licensing Agency Limited, 90 Tottenham Court Road, London, England W1P 0LP. Applications for the copyright owner's written permission to reproduce any part of this publication should be addressed to the publisher.

Warning: The doing of an unauthorised act in relation to a copyright work may result in both a civil claim for damages and criminal prosecution

Preface

This book has been produced primarily to assist the applicant for a JAR Private Pilot's Licence in the study for the Aviation Law and Operational Procedures examination, although it is also intended as a useful reference document for those who have passed the examination. It is not intended as a complete course of study in the subject, but is designed to act as a guide to the main points in the syllabus. It is also a useful general reference for qualified pilots.

In addition, many rules and procedures specific to the UK are covered. These may be printed in *italics* to indicate they are not part of the JAA syllabus, but they are important for flight in the UK, or in UK registered aircraft abroad. As the UK National Private Pilot's Licence is developed, it is anticipated that such UK specific rules and procedures will become part of the syllabus for those examinations.

The most important parts, such as the Rules of the Air, are covered in detail. However, the coverage of parts which the author considers less vital is only sufficient to give a basic understanding of general structure. To cover the whole examination syllabus, and indeed to be sure of complying with the law, all the relevant current official documents need to be studied. Pilots must refer to these documents, if only to check this guide's accuracy, before flight. This is especially true because this guide is not amended as legislation changes.

In this document, the male pronoun 'he' is generally used to refer to both genders. This is no slight on the ladies who fly, merely a space saving and readability measure.

Comments or suggestions on this or any other guides in this series are welcomed.

Editorial Team

Author   David Cockburn

David Cockburn served for many years in the Royal Air Force as a pilot and flying instructor, amassing nearly 6000 flying hours including over 1000 hours instructing on jet trainers and 1000 hours on light piston aeroplanes. During that time he specialised in teaching mainly visual navigation techniques to pilots and navigators in the air and on the ground. He holds a UK Airline Transport Pilots Licence, and since leaving the RAF has worked as a ground instructor in professional flying training schools in this country and abroad, and is the author of several professional training books and manuals. He continues to give flying instruction at flying clubs to PPL and IMC rating students, and is a flight examiner.

Having decided to concentrate on private pilot training, it became apparent that students and private pilots found it difficult to find the practical and important information they needed from the detailed descriptions in the available textbooks. He has therefore produced these guides.

Editor   Daljeet Gill

Daljeet is Head of Design & Development for Pooleys Flight Equipment and editor of the Pooleys Private Pilots Guides, Pre-flight Briefing, R/T Communications, Pooleys ATPL Manuals and Air Presentation, Ground School Training Transparencies plus many others. Daljeet has been involved with editing, typesetting and design for all these publications. Graduated in 1999 with a BA (hons) in Graphic Design, she deals with marketing, advertising & design of our new products. She maintains our website and produces our Pooleys Catalogue annually.

Contents

Chapter 1	Organisations	1
Chapter 2	Airworthiness and Equipment	9
Chapter 3	Licensing	15
Chapter 4	Collision Avoidance	23
Chapter 5	Flight Rules	31
Chapter 6	Signals & Definitions	45
Chapter 7	Airspace	69
Chapter 8	The Aerodrome	87
Chapter 9	Accident Investigation	121
Chapter 10	Search and Rescue	129
	Answers to Exercises	137
	Index	139

INTENTIONALLY LEFT BLANK

Chapter 1

Organisations

1.1 Introduction

The International Civil Aviation Organisation (ICAO) was formed as a result of the Convention on International Civil Aviation, originally signed at Chicago on 7 December 1944 and referred to as the 'Chicago Convention'. The aim of the Convention is that 'international civil aviation may be developed in a safe and orderly manner' It may be interesting to note that it has a further aim, 'that international air transport services may be established on the basis of equality of opportunity and operated soundly and economically'.

1.2 The Chicago Convention

The Convention consists of a series of 'Articles' which express the agreed intentions of the 'Contracting States' *(those which have signed the Convention)*. Once the Articles were agreed, committees drew up 'Annexes to the Convention', which describe how the Articles will be implemented. These Annexes list 'Standards', which the Contracting States agree to make law in their individual countries, and 'Recommended Practices', which they agree should be followed but realise cannot be enforced everywhere. The aim of a 'Recommended Practice' is to raise it to a 'Standard' at a suitable opportunity.

If a State finds it cannot apply a particular Standard, it must file a 'Difference' with ICAO, and list such differences in its own 'Aeronautical Information Publication' or AIP. Each State must publish an AIP containing specific information, such as Controlled and Restricted Airspace and aerodromes which may be used by international aviation, and publish amendments or temporary information in "Notices to Airmen" (NOTAMs).

The Organisation also issues 'Procedures for Air Navigation' (PANS) documents, which expand on certain Annexes, and other documents which provide guidance.

1.3   Sovereignty and Freedoms

The Convention applies over the territory of all the Contracting States, and over the High Seas. Each state has exclusive sovereignty over the airspace above its land territory and adjacent territorial waters. It may make what rules it considers appropriate for flight in that airspace, which all aircraft must obey. It also has the right to require an aircraft flying in its airspace to land there, and the right to search any landing aircraft.

However, each Contracting State agrees to allow civil aircraft of other Contracting States to fly through its airspace, often called the 'first freedom'. They may also land for non-traffic purposes *(eg to take on fuel or make a temporary weather diversion)*, which is the 'second freedom'. Other freedoms allow them to drop or collect passengers, cargo or mail provided they do not carry them between aerodromes within that State *(which is called 'cabotage')*.

These agreed freedoms do not apply to scheduled air transport flights, which are subject to the International Air services Transit Agreement (IATA). For these scheduled flights, each freedom must be individually agreed. There are generally regarded as 5 freedoms. The third freedom allows dropping passengers and freight, the fourth freedom collecting them, and the fifth freedom carrying passengers and freight between that State and a totally different one.

During a flight over the territory of a Contracting State, both the State of Registry *(where the aircraft is registered)*, and the State whose territory is being overflown, have responsibilities to ensure that an aircraft complies with the rules in force. The aircraft *(or to be precise, its operator and its commander)* has a duty to obey the laws of both states.

1.4   Registration

The State of Registry will issue a Certificate of Registration, and a Certificate of Airworthiness which must comply with the Standards in the relevant Annex if the aircraft wish to fly internationally. An aircraft may only be registered in one State at a time. For an international flight, both these certificates must be carried on board. Each aircraft must carry the allocated registration marks displayed on the outside and also inscribed on a plate made of fireproof metal.

1.5   Licensing

Licences issued by any Contracting State which comply fully with the ICAO Annex (the UK ones require additional photographic identification), are accepted in all Contracting States instead of passports. For international flight, each licence must be issued or validated by the State of Registration of the aircraft.

1.6   Facilitation

Customs fees or duty is not to be paid on fuel or oil. Nor is it to be payable on any spares or stores carried on the aircraft and taken back out again. *A practical effect of this is the ability of UK pilots to claim back ("drawback") excise duty on fuel they buy and take out of the country, even to EU states.*

1.7   Other Articles

There are many other regulations which relate directly to air travel. Some of these are only relevant to international travel. Others are expanded in European (JAA) or national regulations. The important ones applying to private aviation, together with Standards and Recommended Practices, are covered specifically here or in other chapters.

1.8 European Regulatory Bodies

Most European States have agreed to work together for the safety of air navigation. Originally formed to co-ordinate aircraft airworthiness requirements, the Joint Aviation Authority (JAA) is the body whose agreed regulations are now becoming law in most of their member States, as well as some others. These Joint Aviation Regulations (JARs) are not legally binding until individual states make them so in their own laws. Licences issued by one JAA state are recognised by all other JAA states, and may be transferred if the holder changes domicile.

The European Union (EU) has legal powers, and their laws apply throughout their member countries. Their "European Aviation Safety Agency" (EASA) oversees aircraft design and maintenance throughout the EU, and is intended to take on further responsibilities in future. However, several JAA states are not members of the EU, and because EU legislation is exceedingly cumbersome, the JARs have been incorporated in UK law as part of our own Air Navigation Order.

Eurocontrol is a body which co-ordinates Air Traffic Control over large areas of the continent, mainly in upper airspace.

The European Council for Air Co-operation (ECAC) is a broader body which works to reduce differences in laws and procedures between member states.

1.9 UK Law

Flight in the United Kingdom is subject to the Air Navigation Order (ANO), which contains the Statutory Instruments passed by Parliament and which is the way in which ICAO Standards and Recommended Practices (SARPs) and JARs have legal effect in our country. It also includes rules which are 'differences' from ICAO Standards. Attached to the ANO are the Rules of the Air Regulations and Air Navigation (General) Regulations, both of which also have legal status. The Air Navigation (Noise Certification) Order applies to virtually every aircraft except those which have very short take-off and landing characteristics. In addition, the Restriction of Flying Regulations, and certain local by-laws and statutory instruments, apply to flight over parts of the UK, and these must also be obeyed. Apart from the Noise Regulations and local by-laws, all of these are contained in Civil Aviation Publication (CAP) 393.

The Air Navigation Order applies to all aircraft registered in the UK, wherever they may be at the time. It has two sections. The Articles lay down the basic requirements, and the Schedules expand on the articles in detail. For instance, Article 21 of the Order states that a pilot requires a licence. Schedule 8 details the privileges and requirements of each type of licence and rating. Many of the Articles start by specifically referring to public transport flights, but some of these have parts which apply to all flights.

One of the important Articles (Art 43) of the ANO describes the aircraft commander's responsibilities to "reasonably satisfy himself" before flight that that flight can be made safely. This not only means that he must check that all the rules have been (and are planned to be) complied with, but also implies he must use the knowledge and judgement which he demonstrated in the licensing examinations which he has passed. Basically, unless there is a specific rule elsewhere, "the buck stops with the pilot".

In addition to the AIP, the UK also publishes a series of Aeronautical Informational Circulars (AICs), which contain additional information and guidance. Like the AIP, AICs are published on the web site of the Aeronautical Information Service www.ais.org.uk. AICs are divided into information on Restrictions of Flying Regulations (printed on mauve paper), safety (pink), aeronautical charts (green) operational (yellow) and administrative information (white).

INTENTIONALLY LEFT BLANK

1.10 Exercise

1. On an international flight, which documents do ICAO require to be carried in the aircraft?

    a. The Certificate of Airworthiness only
    b. The Certificate of Registration only
    c. The Certificate of Registration and the Certificate of Airworthiness
    d. No documents are specifically required

2. Under the Chicago Convention, who is responsible for the laws which an international aircraft arriving or departing a member state of the European Union must obey?

    a. ICAO
    b. The State of Registry
    c. The European Parliament
    c. The State which is being visited

3. The Chicago Convention allows aircraft registered in Contracting States to fly over other Contracting States' territory without specific permission. Which of the following is correct?

    a. All aircraft may fly over all other states' territory at all times
    b. All civil aircraft may fly over all other states' territory at all times
    c. Only non-scheduled civil aircraft may fly over without prior permission
    d. All civil aircraft may only fly over other states' territory if they land there

4. The pilot of an aircraft on an international flight must hold a licence issued or validated by:

    a. the state from which the aircraft took off?
    b. the state where the aircraft is based?
    c. the state where the aircraft is registered?
    d. any contracting state?

5. As defined in the Chicago Convention, a State's territory over which it has sovereignty includes:

   a. Only the land areas which are part of the State
   b. Only the inhabited land areas which are part of that State
   c. The total land areas plus the adjacent territorial waters
   d. The total land areas plus only the territorial waters out to 6 nm

6. Which of the following does the Chicago Convention exempt from customs duty?

   a. Lubricating oils which are in the aircraft tanks or sumps only
   b. Lubricating oils which remain on board the aircraft only
   c. Lubricating oils and spare parts which remain on board only
   d. Lubricating oils and spare parts which are exported on the next flight only

7. The Air Navigation Order applies to:

   a. All UK registered aircraft, wherever they are
   b. All UK registered aircraft in UK airspace only
   c. All UK registered aircraft, in UK airspace or over the high seas
   d. All aircraft in UK airspace only

8. Which national documents list a state's differences from ICAO Standards?

   a. The ANO only
   b. The AIP only
   c. The ANO and NOTAMs
   d. The AIP and NOTAMs

Chapter 2

Airworthiness & Equipment

2.1 Airworthiness

An aircraft registered in the UK cannot normally fly without a valid Certificate of Airworthiness (C of A), issued by the European Aviation Safety Agency (EASA), the UK Civil Aviation Authority (CAA) or another document equating to a C of A and issued by an organisation approved by the CAA. A 'full' or 'ICAO compliant' C of A gives all the international privileges laid down by ICAO. However, some limitations may be placed on the C of A, and any C of A with restrictions does not automatically allow the aircraft to fly over other states. The pilot of such an aircraft, or one with only a 'Permit to Fly' requires positive permission from any state in whose airspace he wishes to fly.

Initially, the type of aircraft (for example a Slingsby T-67) must be tested under the supervision of approved surveyors and test pilots. If satisfactory, a 'Type Approval' is issued. Thereafter, each individual aircraft has its own C of A issued after careful inspection of the relevant aircraft. A UK C of A will specify the type of operations for which the aircraft may be used (for example, 'private' or 'transport' category).

The C of A will state the conditions and limitations in which the aircraft is considered airworthy. These are stated in the Flight Manual, which forms part of the C of A, and the limitations are repeated on placards in the cockpit. Part III of the ANO lays down the UK law on airworthiness and equipment of aircraft.

2.2 Maintenance

Any work carried out on the aircraft will invalidate the C of A unless it is carried out in an approved manner, with approved materials. From time to time, EASA or the CAA may issue mandatory modifications or require inspections to be carried out. Unless these are carried out as required, the C of A becomes invalid. It is also invalid if the routine inspections which are required as part of an approved maintenance schedule are not carried out.

The daily Check 'A' included in the LAMS *(see below)* is one of these inspections, and can be carried out by a licensed pilot. A Check 'A' is valid for 24 hours.

On an aircraft certificated in the UK 'transport' (applies to remunerated flying training) or 'aerial work' categories, or one used for such purposes, all work must be inspected and given a 'Certificate of Maintenance Review' by an engineer licensed by the CAA (or JAA). For aircraft below 2750 kg certificated in the 'private' or 'special' category, the owner (if he holds a pilot's licence) may carry out certain work himself without involving a licensed engineer, but he must record the details in the aircraft log book. Every aircraft must have a Certificate of Maintenance Review signed at the intervals laid down in the maintenance schedule, which must be approved by the certificating body (EASA or CAA), but if (as in the case of many light aircraft) no specific approved manufacturer's schedule is available, the generic Light Aircraft Maintenance Schedule (LAMS), issued by the CAA itself, may be used.

The LAMS (and the ANO) lists the repairs which may be carried out by a pilot/owner, which are limited to those which do not affect the aircraft's primary structure or controls. For example, replacing tyres, most light bulbs, or removable parts such as cowlings or wheel spats are included. Refuelling and oil replenishment of any aircraft, not just in the private category, may be carried out by a licensed crew member.

Aircraft certificated in the transport or aerial work category, or used for such operations, must have a formal technical log kept. Entries must be made by the commander as soon as practicable after flight. These entries include the times of take-off and landing, and any defects which affect the aircraft's airworthiness. Rectification of these defects will include a 'Certificate of Release to Service' signed by a licensed engineer. The technical log must be carried in all relevant aircraft unless they are landing back at the same aerodrome as they departed, and are not flying across an international boundary.

All aircraft must be weighed and a weight schedule must be prepared by the operator. The schedule must be kept for a period of 6 months after the next weighing.

2.3 Mandatory Equipment

The ANO Schedule 4 lays down the equipment which all aircraft must carry in flight. For most private light aeroplanes the requirements are as follows, helicopters have slightly different rules:

- Spare fuses for all electrical fuses which can be replaced in flight (minimum 3 of each rating)
- Maps, charts and other documents and navigation equipment for the route and possible diversion
- Safety belts for every seat in use, with shoulder harnesses except for rear seats of old aircraft

For night flight, the following must also be carried:

- Aircraft lights as described in chapter 4
- Lighting for reading the instruments and safety
- Signalling light if no radio is fitted
- A sensitive altimeter adjustable for pressure datums
- A Turn & slip indicator or gyroscopic attitude and direction indicators

For aerobatics:

- A safety harness for every seat, whether in use or not

For flight under IFR (see Chapter 5) outside controlled airspace:

- A sensitive altimeter adjustable for pressure datums
- A Turn & slip indicator or gyroscopic attitude and direction indicators

For flight over water there are no legal requirements. However, lifejackets should be worn by all occupants of single engined aircraft whenever the aircraft flies out of gliding range of the shore, and liferafts should be carried if the aircraft is more than 100 nm from shore.

2.4 Documentation for International Flight

Certain documents must be carried under UK law by all aircraft, including private flights, when flying internationally, and these are listed here.

- The crew's licences
- The Certificate of Airworthiness
- The Certificate of Registration
- The licence for the aircraft radio
- A copy of the international rules for intercepting and intercepted aircraft (see chapter 5)

2.5 Noise Certificates

UK registered aircraft must possess a valid noise certificate, issued by the CAA. If such a certificate contains specific requirements, these must be complied with. The noise requirements for the issue of such a certificate are laid down in the Air Navigation (Noise Certification) Order 1990.

2.6 Pilot's Responsibilities

It is the pilot's responsibility to check before flight that the aircraft is fit for flight, and that any necessary maintenance paperwork has been completed. He is also responsible for ensuring that any required equipment is carried and serviceable.

2.7 Exercise

1. A UK private category Certificate of Airworthiness is not valid:

    a. until the Check 'A' is signed in the technical log
    b. if the pilot makes any repairs to his aircraft such as changing the wheel
    c. if the aircraft is repaired or modified except in the approved manner
    d. in all the above cases

2. The ANO requires all private light aircraft to carry certain items at all times. Which are these?

    a. Spare fuses, life jackets for all occupants and charts for the route
    b. Navigation lights, charts for the route and safety belts for all occupants
    c. Charts for the route, spare fuses and safety belts for all occupants
    d. Navigation lights, charts for the route, safety belts and lifejackets for all occupants

3. In addition to the items at question 2, which of the following must be carried by a UK registered private light aircraft on an international flight?

    a. The Certificate of Airworthiness and Certificate of Registration only
    b. The C of A, Certificate of Registration and the crew's licences
    c. The C of A, Certificate of Registration, crew's licences and radio licence
    d. The C of A, Certificate of Registration, crew's & radio licences and interception procedures.

4. Where would you find the flight limitations which apply to an aircraft's Certificate of Airworthiness?

    a. In the Maintenance Schedule only
    b. In the Flight Manual only
    c. In the Maintenance Schedule and the technical log
    d. In the Flight Manual and on cockpit placards

INTENTIONALLY LEFT BLANK

Chapter 3

Licensing

3.1 Introduction

ICAO requires the pilot of an aircraft to hold a licence issued or validated by the State of Registry of the aircraft. Validation means accepting a licence issued by another state, and certifying that it is valid in your own state.

Part IV of the ANO requires that no person may basically do anything to an aircraft registered in the UK unless he or she holds a valid licence issued by the CAA or JAA. To fly it, he needs a pilot's licence. To certify its airworthiness, he needs an engineer's licence. To give a pilot instructions, he needs an Air Traffic Controller's licence. To give a pilot information necessary for flight safety, he needs a Flight Information Service Officer's licence. To operate a radio, he needs a Radio Telephonist's licence, for ground or airborne transmissions. This chapter only deals with the licences and associated ratings which affect a private pilot.

3.2 The Pilot

It must be remembered that the pilot is the commander of the aircraft, and responsible for almost everything to do with the flight. He must satisfy himself that the aircraft is airworthy by checking the technical log and ensuring the Certificate of Maintenance Review is valid. He is responsible for ensuring the aircraft has enough fuel for the proposed flight, and that he carries those items which the ANO requires him to carry, such as up-to-date charts. He is also responsible for ensuring that the weather is not only fit for the flight, but provides sufficient performance for safe take-off and landing on the intended runway. He is also responsible for ensuring that the aircraft is safely loaded.

In flight, he is responsible for complying with any ATC clearance. He must also obey the Rules of the Air, and any other regulations, even if ATC give him instructions which conflict with these Rules. For example, he may not fly a single engined aircraft over a congested area unless he can glide clear in the event of an engine failure, even if ATC gives him a clearance. (However, some rules may be waived by ATC clearances, such as the requirement to maintain a minimum of 1500 feet above that congested area). He must also comply with any Restriction of Flying Regulations as published in AICs and NOTAMs, which means he must study these before flight. These are available at most aerodromes, and as explained in chapter 1 are published on the UK Aeronautical Services' web site (at the time of writing www.ais.org.uk).

3.3 The Student Pilot

Although Article 21 of the ANO requires that no person may act as a member of the crew of an aircraft unless he or she holds a valid licence, persons over 16 years old with a valid medical certificate may act as pilot in command under the authorisation of a flying instructor, provided no-one else is in the aircraft.

3.4 The JAR Medical

The JAR medical certificate, which forms part of the licence which a student wishes to gain, must be issued by an authorised medical examiner (AME) in accordance with JAR FCL-3 (Medical). For private flight in light aircraft, a JAA Class 2 medical certificate is enough (Class 1 is required for professional pilots). The certificate is only valid while the pilot is healthy.

If a pilot is aware of any decrease in his medical fitness, JAR-FCL 3.040 requires him to seek the advice of the CAA without undue delay when becoming aware of:

- hospital or clinic admission for more than 12 hours
- surgical operation or 'invasive procedure'
- regular use of medication
- regular use of correcting lenses

As laid down on the certificate itself, he or she must inform the CAA or an AME of any of the following, when the medical certificate will be regarded as 'suspended':

- any significant personal injury involving incapacity to function as a pilot
- a 21 day period of illness involving incapacity to function as a pilot
- being pregnant

3.5 Requirements for the JAR PPL

The requirements for the JAR PPL are laid down in JAR - FCL 1 (Aeroplanes) or JAR-FCL 3 (Helicopters) as appropriate. The licence, which is valid for 5 years, allows a person to act as pilot in command of any aircraft type or class for which he holds a valid rating, and to carry passengers. In certain cases, he may tow gliders or drop parachutists, but may not receive any remuneration for that or for any flight. He must maintain competency by meeting the requirements of JAR-FCL.

To gain the PPL, a person must pass a series of ground examinations with a ground examiner, complete a minimum of 45 hours of airborne time, including at least 25 hours in dual training of specific exercises, and at least 10 hours solo under the supervision of a flight instructor, and pass a skill test with a flight examiner. The training must be carried out by a Registered Training Facility in a JAA member state, although dispensations may be granted to train in other states.

3.6 Requirements for a JAR Class or Type Rating

The holder of a pilot's licence may not fly as pilot-in-command of an aircraft unless his licence contains a valid class or type rating appropriate to the aircraft being flown.

To obtain a rating which allows him to fly a particular type or class of aircraft, a pilot must pass a skill test on an aircraft of that type or class. Most aircraft used for single engine PPL training are in the Single Engined Piston (land) aeroplane class [SEP (land)]. In order to fly a type or class which was not included in the original skill test for the licence issue, a pilot must pass a further skill test on the new type or class. Complex aeroplanes in the SEP class require "differences training" before the pilot may exercise his rating privileges on that type.

Multi-engined classes or types require specific training at a Flying Training Organisation.

3.7 UK National PPL

In parallel with the JAA procedures, the UK (or any country) may issue a National PPL which has different training, testing, and medical requirements. Such a national licence is only valid within the boundaries of the State which issues it, although other states may recognise it for certain purposes if they so wish.

The National licence is not part of the JAR system, and does not officially count towards any JAR licence which a pilot may wish to obtain in the future. There is such a UK National PPL, whose associated administrative procedures are the responsibility of the National Pilot Licensing Group (NPLG), or whichever recognised Association the pilot wishes to sponsor his licence. The CAA issues the licence on their recommendation.

The medical requirements are totally different. The pilot signs a statement that he does not suffer from any illness which could prevent him holding a pilot's licence. The pilot's own General Practitioner doctor, who holds the pilot's medical records, then signs the form to certify that the pilot is indeed fit to hold a licence. There are 2 standards of medical certificate under the national scheme. The first standard equates to that for a heavy goods vehicle driver, and allows the holder to carry passengers. The second standard, which allows only solo flight or flight with another qualified pilot, is equivalent to that for a private driving licence.

Other limits apply to a holder of the UK National PPL (Aeroplanes). The largest "simple single-engined aeroplane" which he may fly as pilot-in-command is one with a maximum take-off weight authorised of 2000 kg, with a maximum of 4 occupants. He must remain in a flight visibility of at least 5 kilometres, and may not fly at night, in IMC or any other circumstances which require him to comply with the instrument flight rules (see following chapters).

3.8   Instrument Meteorological Conditions Rating

The IMC rating is unique to the UK, and is a national or 'special purpose' rating which may be added to a UK or JAA licence. Its privileges only apply in the UK, although it is theoretically possible for other states to recognise it if specifically requested.

The IMC rating allows holders to fly out of sight of the ground and in IMC outside (and even inside some) controlled airspace. It also allows them to fly under Visual Flight Rules (VFR, see Chapter 5) in flight visibility less than 3000 metres (when below 3000 feet and flying at less than 140 knots).

If carrying out 'simulated' instrument flight training at any time, the aircraft must be fitted with dual controls and a safety pilot must be carried to assist, especially with look-out.

3.9 Revalidation

Revalidation means extending the privileges of a licence or rating for a further period, which must be done before the original expires. To revalidate a JAR *or UK National PPL*, only the ratings must be revalidated. To revalidate a JAR SEP rating on a single pilot aircraft, which is valid for 2 years, a pilot must pass a proficiency check with a flight examiner within the last 3 months of the rating's original validity. Alternatively, he may "re-validate by experience", having done the following in an aircraft of the same class:

- Flown at least 12 hours in the last 12 months
- Flown at least 6 hours in the last 12 months as pilot in command
- Made at least 12 take-offs and landings in the last 12 months
- Flown 1 hour with a flight instructor within the last 12 months

At the time of writing, no signature is required to revalidate the SEP (or 'SSEA') rating for a National PPL (Aeroplanes), but the pilot must maintain "rolling validity" by continually ensuring he has flown 6 hours in a simple single engined aeroplane (SSEA), including 4 as pilot in command, in the 12 months preceding the flight he wishes to undertake. He must also have carried out a training flight with a flying instructor within the previous 24 months. However, it is probable that these requirements will change, and readers must consult the latest version of the ANO (or the CAA's book 'LASORS') to determine current requirements.

3.10 Renewal

If a pilot is unable to revalidate a rating, and it lapses, he must renew it by passing a relevant proficiency test. He may also be required to undergo a certain amount of training.

3.11 Licence Privileges

In the UK, Schedule 8 to the Air Navigation Order lays out the privileges of licences and places restrictions on PPL holders. Among the main restrictions are that an aeroplane PPL holder may not receive any remuneration for his services as a pilot, that he cannot fly at night without a night qualification, *and that the holder of a UK-issued PPL without a valid IMC or Instrument Rating must remain at all times in sight of the surface and in a flight visibility (see chapter 5) of at least 3 kilometres.*

Pilots may not carry passengers unless in the period of 90 days beforehand they have carried out 3 take-offs and landings as sole manipulator of the controls (handling pilot). To carry passengers at night, at least one of these 3 take-offs and landings must have been at night. Night is defined as from 30 minutes after sunset (end of evening civil twilight) to 30 minutes before sunrise (beginning of morning civil twilight), measured at the surface.

3.12 Flight Time

Flight time is defined as the time between the aircraft first moving for the purpose of becoming airborne to coming to rest after landing. This is usually referred to as 'chock-to-chock' or 'brakes to brakes' time. For flight time to count towards gaining, revalidating, or renewing a rating, it must be flown in an aircraft of the same class or type as appropriate. All dual, solo or pilot-in-command time which the pilot is entitled to log, counts in full towards requirements for the licence or rating.

3.13 Exercise

1. How long is a JAA private pilot's licence valid?

   a. 12 months
   b. 24 months
   c. 36 months
   d. 60 months

2. How long must an operator keep the weighing schedule?

   a. 6 months after the weighing
   b. When the next weight schedule is completed
   c. 6 months after the next weight schedule is completed
   d. 12 months after the weighing

3. A pilot who wishes to carry passengers must have flown 3 take-offs and landings within a certain period before the flight. What is that period?

   a. 6 months
   b. 90 days
   c. 60 days
   d. 30 days

4. When a pilot hires an aircraft from a Flying Club, who is responsible for ensuring that the (i) weather is suitable, and (ii) the aircraft is airworthy?

   a. (i) the pilot-in-command   (ii) The owner
   b. (i) The CFI   (ii) The owner
   c. (i) the pilot-in-command   (ii) The CFI
   d. (i) the pilot-in-command   (ii) The pilot-in-command

5. What is the definition of 'night'?

   a. From sunset to sunrise
   b. From 30 minutes before sunset to 30 minutes after sunrise
   c. From the beginning of evening civil twilight to the end of morning civil twilight
   d. From the end of evening civil twilight to the beginning of morning civil twilight

6. Where is the IMC rating valid if attached to a JAA licence?

   a. In any ICAO Contracting State
   b. In any JAA State
   c. In the UK only
   d. Nowhere

7. What should a pilot do if he falls ill and is unfit to fly?

   a. Inform the CAA immediately
   b. Inform the CAA or any AME immediately
   c. Inform the CAA within 21 days
   d. Inform the CAA or any AME if he is still unfit after 21 days

8. How many hours (i) dual and (ii) solo must a PPL applicant have before he may apply for a JAR PPL?

   a. (i) 20 hours   (ii) 20 hours
   b. (i) 25 hours   (ii) 15 hours
   c. (i) 20 hours   (ii) 10 hours
   d. (i) 25 hours   (ii) 10 hours

9. Where can a pilot read the privileges of his JAA PPL?

   a. In the licence itself
   b. In a schedule to the ANO
   c. In the AIP
   d. In an Annex to the Chicago Convention

Chapter 4

Collision Avoidance

4.1 Introduction

ICAO Annex 2 lays down the internationally agreed rules which must be obeyed at all times in order to avoid collisions. These are split into General Rules, Visual Flight Rules, and Instrument Flight Rules. This chapter contains the General Rules and it and the two following give those rules most relevant to light aircraft pilots. Those in *italics* are not ICAO rules, but apply to all aircraft in United Kingdom airspace.

4.2 Risk of Collision

The right of way rules given below strictly only apply if there is a risk of collision, although they are also useful guidance to maintain safe separation between aircraft. A risk of collision exists if the two aircraft appear to stay in the same relative position to each other; in other words if the pilot of one sees the other apparently staying in the same position in the windscreen. (While the pilot is watching the other aircraft, his eyes do not have to move to follow it.)

4.3 Right of Way in the Air

a. General Rules

If there is a risk of collision between two or more aircraft, at least one must 'give way' (change its path to allow the other to continue). An aircraft with the 'right of way' is to maintain its course and speed. However, nothing takes away a pilot's responsibility for the safety of his aircraft, so if the other pilot is not giving way he should take whatever action he thinks best to avoid a collision. An aircraft giving way is not to pass above or below the other, but must keep clear of it. A landing aircraft has right of way over all others.

b. Head on approaches

If two aircraft are approaching each other head-on, and there is a risk of collision, both must alter course to the right. No-one has right of way.

c. Overtaking

An aircraft overtaking another must alter its course to the right, and must keep clear of the one being overtaken.

d. Converging priority

If there is a risk of collision, but the aircraft are in neither a head-on nor an overtaking situation, the principle is that the more manoeuvrable aircraft must give way to those less manoeuvrable at all times. Therefore the types of aircraft are listed in order of priority, as follows:

1. Balloons
2. Gliders
3. Airships
4. Flying machines ('power-driven heavier than air craft' = aeroplanes & helicopters)

This means that an aeroplane (or helicopter) must give way to any other type of aircraft. In addition, aeroplanes towing gliders have priority over airships and flying machines.

e. Converging actions

When two aircraft with similar priority are approaching each other on converging courses, and there is a risk of collision, the aircraft with the other one on its right must give way. As in both the previous examples, the method of giving way is to be a turn to the right, which in this case should ensure the aircraft giving way passes behind the other.

4.4 Right of Way on the Ground

a. General

Rules for giving way are similar for those in the air. However, instead of altering course, it is usually more appropriate for the aircraft giving way to stop. The only difference in giving way is that an aircraft overtaking another on the ground must alter its course to the LEFT. *However, in the UK an aircraft lining up beside another for take-off on an airfield without runways must line up on the other's right.*

b. Priorities

For an aircraft on the ground, the priorities are as follows, starting with the highest and with no regard for the priority of aircraft types in paragraph 4.3 above, which only applies in the air.

- Aircraft landing
- Aircraft taking off
- Vehicles towing aircraft
- Aircraft taxiing
- Vehicles

4.5 Landing

An aircraft landing has right of way over all other traffic. If two or more aircraft are landing, ATC (if they exist) will allocate priorities. If there is no ATC, or ATC has not allocated a priority, the lower aircraft has the right of way. However, if a pilot knows that another aircraft has an emergency which compels it to land, he must give way to it.

a. Runway Use

*In the United Kingdom, aircraft may **not** land on a runway if another aircraft is already on it. However, as a **special case**, at an airfield with ATC, the **controller** may give permission for a pilot to land if certain requirements are met. No other person may give such permission.*

b. Grass Airfields

*If there are marked runways, the rules above apply. However, if there are no marked runways, it is permitted for an aircraft to land to one side of another which has already landed. The landing pilot must land **to the right** of the one which has already landed. As a logical extension of that rule, after landing on such an aerodrome, all pilots must **turn left after landing** to check behind.*

4.6 Lights Carried by Aircraft

a. Conspicuity Lights

Most types of aircraft, including all aeroplanes, are required to show anti-collision beacons (either red or white) at any time when the engine is running. It is also advisable to show landing lights when flying at low level, to give warning of one's presence to birds as well as other aircraft.

b. Navigation Lights

All aircraft have to show navigation lights at night (between twilights - 30 minutes after sunset to 30 minutes before sunrise, as measured on the ground). Balloons show a red light below the basket, and other aircraft show the lights as described below, although gliders have the choice of showing the lights below or a single red light shining in all directions.

The picture shows an aircraft from above. The lights displayed must be visible from directly above to directly below the aircraft, over a horizontal area bounded by the lines shown. The green light on the starboard (right) side shines from directly ahead of the aircraft round to 110° from the direction of flight. The red light shines over a similar arc on the left (port) side. The white light shines over an arc 70° either side of the aircraft's tail, covering a total angle of 140°. (This angle defines the "overtaking" bracket for the Rules of the Air). An observer can calculate the approximate heading of an aircraft whose navigation lights are visible to him.

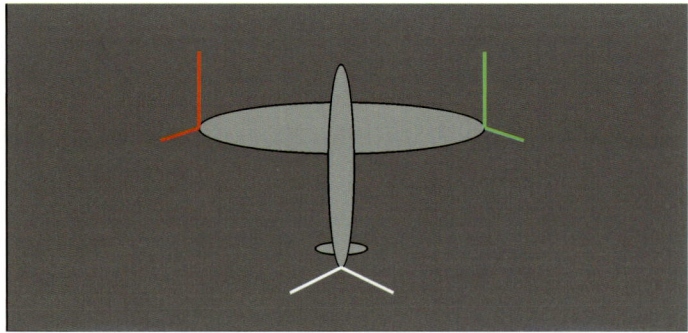

FIGURE 4.1 NAVIGATION LIGHTS

The navigation lights allow a simplification of the right of way rules at night. If a pilot sees a navigation light which is not moving relative to him, there is a risk of collision. If the light is green, he has right of way. If the light is red, he must give way by altering course to the right. If he sees both red and green the other aircraft is approaching head on and he must alter course to the right. If the light is white, he is overtaking and must alter course to the right.

Examination questions often involve positions in which lights become visible, and require answers about the correct actions to be taken. A red light seen on a pilot's left, for example, would not remain in the same relative position, and would require no action. Relative bearings (360 degrees around the aircraft's heading) may be referred to in questions.

INTENTIONALLY LEFT BLANK

4.7 Exercise

1. When must a pilot normally show his anti-collision beacon?

    a. At all times when he is in the aircraft
    b. At all times when the aircraft engines are running
    c. From take-off to landing
    d. There is no requirement to show such a beacon

2. What colour navigation light would a pilot see on an aircraft which he is overtaking at night?

    a. Red
    b. Yellow
    c. Green
    d. White

3. To which of the following must the pilot of a helicopter give way if it is on a converging course with him and there is a risk of collision?

    a. A balloon only
    b. A glider or a balloon
    c. A glider, a balloon or an airship
    d. A glider, a balloon, an airship or an aeroplane towing a glider

4. The pilot of an aircraft which has the right of way must do certain things to reduce the risk of collision. Apart from monitoring the other aircraft' actions, what else must he do?

    a. Maintain heading, speed, and altitude
    b. Maintain heading and altitude only
    c. Maintain altitude and speed only
    d. Maintain heading and speed only

5. Under what circumstances should an aircraft giving way alter its course to the left?

    a. At all times
    b. Only when overtaking in the air
    c. Only when overtaking on the ground
    d. Never

6. An aircraft is landing on an airfield without designated runways in the UK. Another aircraft has already landed. On which side of the other aircraft must the landing pilot land?

    a. Its left
    b. Its right
    c. He must not land with another aircraft on the manoeuvring area
    d. He must await instructions from a FISO

7. A pilot sees only a red navigation light as his level at night.
What could that represent?

    a. An aeroplane with a failed anti-collision beacon to which he must give way
    b. A glider
    c. A free balloon
    d. Any of the above

Chapter 5

Flight Rules

5.1 Introduction

This chapter continues the guidance on ICAO Annex 2, which is entitled 'Rules of the Air' and basically lays down the Visual and Instrument Flight Rules, when they are applicable, and what they are. It also details various other rules which concern the pilot while he is flying, and several definitions. It should be noted that the Rules of the Air in Annex 2 **apply to all aircraft** of every signatory nation, no matter where they may fly, unless they conflict with the laws of the state over which it is flying. It also applies **over the high seas everywhere.** They are United Kingdom law and are published in CAP 393.

There are also United Kingdom 'differences' which have been notified to ICAO and which are included here in italics. These 'differences' are also UK law.

5.2 What are Flight Rules?

These are the rules which a pilot must obey in order to **avoid collisions.** They are nothing to do with how he is flying the aircraft. The **General Rules** he must follow at all times in the air, and on an airfield manoeuvring area, have been described in chapter 4. In addition, in the air, he must follow either **Visual Flight Rules** (VFR) or **Instrument Flight Rules** (IFR). If he is following the Visual Flight Rules, he must use his eyes to avoid collision with other aircraft. If he is following the Instrument Flight Rules, he is using an instrument to achieve the same result. However, nothing absolves him from his primary responsibility, of using all available information to avoid collisions.

In most cases, the choice of which of the two sets of Rules to follow lies with the **pilot in command.** He has **final authority** as to the disposition of the aircraft, and determines which set of rules are most suitable at the time.

For example, a commercial pilot will usually opt for IFR, as offering the maximum safety for his flight, but on occasion he may wish to follow VFR. Conversely, a private pilot will usually prefer the flexibility offered by VFR, but the ATS (Air Traffic Services) authority may require him to fly under IFR. It is the **responsibility** of the pilot in command to obey whichever Rules he chooses or is required to follow, although he may deviate from the Rules if he considers it **essential in the interests of safety.**

5.3 Visual Flight Rules

Basically, if a pilot opts to follow the Visual Flight Rules, he uses his eyes to avoid other aircraft and the ground, and obey the laws of the state in which he is flying. To do that, he must be able to see aircraft and obstructions. That means visibility must be adequate, and he must stay away from cloud both horizontally and vertically. The minimum flight visibility, distance from cloud, and cloud ceiling, form the **Visual Meteorological Conditions** or **VMC**, also sometimes referred to as the 'VFR minima'.

5.4 Visual Meteorological Conditions

VMC vary depending on the class of airspace in which the aircraft is flying (see chapter 7) and its altitude (or Flight Level). Basically, the pilot must stay **more than 1500 metres** horizontally and **1000 feet** vertically away from cloud, and at high altitudes he must have a **flight visibility** (visibility forward from the cockpit) of **8 km** or more.

When **below 10,000 feet**, the minimum flight visibility drops to **5 km.** In class F or G airspace (see Chapter 7) **at or below 3000 feet** the option exists for the national ATS authority to allow minimum visibilities of as low as 1500 metres. Helicopters may be allowed to operate in less than 1500 metres visibility if manoeuvred at a low speed. At or below 3000 feet the cloud separation minima drop to merely staying clear of cloud, but pilots must stay in sight of the surface. The cloud separation rule in class B airspace is also merely to stay **clear of cloud**, because ATC (Air Traffic Control) there provide a separation service to all aircraft.

In VMC, the pilot in command has the **option** of flying under either VFR or IFR, unless the ATS authority decrees that he must obey IFR. Table 1 below lays out the various VMC **minima** for the different classes of airspace.

Class	A	B	C	D	E	F	G
Vertical cloud separation	NO VMC	Clear of cloud	300 m / 1000 ft			300m / 1000 ft **or if at or below 3000 ft** clear of cloud & in sight of surface	
Horizontal cloud separation		Clear of cloud	1500 ft			1500 m **or if at or below 3000 ft** clear of cloud	
Minimum Flight Visibility		8 km at or above 10000 ft 5 km below 10000 ft				8 km at or above 10000 ft 5 km below 10000 ft (*or as in para 5.4*)	

Table 1

*In the UK, **below 3000 feet amsl**, VFR flight is also allowed in the following circumstances:*

- *For aircraft other than helicopters at or below 140 knots, class C, D, or E airspace - Clear of cloud and in sight of the surface, visibility 5 km or more.*
- *For aircraft other than helicopters at or below 140 knots, class F or G airspace - Clear of cloud and in sight of the surface, visibility 1500 metres or more.*
- *For helicopters, class C, D, E, F or G airspace - Clear of cloud and in sight of the surface, minimum visibility commensurate with speed.*

The UK has no class C airspace at present, and all class B airspace is above FL245.

Licence privileges and restrictions prevent most PPL holders from flying in low flight visibility. See chapter 3, paragraph 3.11.

5.5 Ground Avoidance under VFR

Annex 2 lays down certain responsibilities for avoiding the ground and inconveniencing others. Except **when necessary** during takeoff and landing (that includes the initial climb and the traffic pattern), VFR aircraft must not fly below **500 feet** above ground or water. When over congested areas (including "settlements"), or over large groups of people, they must not fly below **1000 feet** above the highest **obstacle within 600 metres** of the aircraft's flight path. An ATS authority may authorise lesser separation. However, the General Rules also state that all aircraft flying over such congested areas or assemblies must do so at a height allowing a **safe landing** away from the area without undue hazard to anyone on the ground, and ATS have **no authority** to waive that rule.

In the UK, the Rules of the Air Regulations lay down slightly different rules which do not mention ground avoidance at all! According to Rule 5 of the Rules of the Air, contained with the ANO in CAP 393, pilots must not come closer to any person, vessel, vehicle or structure than 500 feet (unless taking off or landing or a glider slope soaring). Over a congested area, they must fly higher than 1500 feet above the highest fixed object within 2000 feet of the aircraft (which can be waived by ATC if necessary), and must be able to land clear of the congested area in the event of engine failure (even if ATC give contrary instructions). An aircraft must not fly over or within 3000 feet of an assembly of more than 1000 people without written permission, and must always be able to glide clear of that assembly.

5.6 VFR Restrictions

Unless the appropriate ATS authority allows, VFR flight is not allowed either above **FL200**, (see para 5.9 for an explanation of 'FL') or at **transonic and supersonic** speeds. The ATS authority may not allow VFR flight in RVSM (reduced vertical separation minima) airspace, where IFR vertical separation remains 1000 feet between FL290 and FL410 (see para 5.11). Perhaps we could clarify here that an ATS **authority** is the authority designated by the State to provide air traffic services in the airspace, whereas an ATC **unit** can be considered to be the individual controller of the aircraft at the time.

In the UK, there is no specific altitude restriction on VFR flight outside controlled airspace. However, VFR flight is not allowed at night (but see para 5.8), nor below FL100 at airspeeds above 250 knots. (The speed restriction also applies to IFR traffic except in class A, B, or C airspace.)

5.7 Cruising Altitudes under Visual Flight Rules

Pilots who are following VFR in level flight outside controlled airspace (CAS, see chapter 7) and above 3000 feet (or more if nationally specified) are to cruise at certain altitudes to reduce the risk of collision. These altitudes are similar but **500 feet higher** than the altitudes for IFR flight detailed below in paragraph 5.11, and are shown in figure 5.2.

The UK again has a difference here. Because of the shape of the country, we have chosen to use a 'quadrantal' IFR cruising system, and so no levels are available specifically for VFR flight. VFR flights in the UK are recommended to use IFR levels. However, UK pilots flying abroad will be expected to use VFR levels.

5.8 VFR Flight in Controlled Airspace

VFR cruising levels in controlled airspace are the same as IFR levels detailed in para 5.11. VFR flights must also comply with the General Rules; submit a **flight plan, obtain** and **comply** with ATC **clearances** in the air and on the ground, listen out on the appropriate frequency, and make position reports. Listening and making **position reports** also applies in Advisory Airspace if the aircraft is using the advisory service. In addition, VFR flights are forbidden in the traffic pattern or Aerodrome Traffic Zone (ATZ) of an airfield inside Controlled Airspace unless the cloud ceiling is at or above **1500 feet** and ground visibility is **5 km** or more. However, ATC may allow flights in worse conditions by permitting the flight to take place under 'Special VFR', which is a VFR flight cleared by Air Traffic Control to operate within a control zone in specific meteorological conditions below the VMC laid down for that class of airspace.

Again in the UK there is no requirement for VFR flights in controlled airspace to use any specific cruising altitudes or levels. They would normally be expected to use the IFR levels.

A pilot can request a Special VFR clearance (which may be granted at night) in controlled airspace in the UK without filing a formal flight plan; brief details of the proposed flight should be passed to the appropriate ATC unit. A flight under Special VFR must remain clear of cloud and in sight of the surface; more stringent conditions apply in each Control Zone.

5.9 Altimeter Settings

A pressure altimeter indicates vertical distance (in feet) above whatever datum point the pilot selects. The pilot selects the datum by changing the pressure set on the altimeter sub-scale. If the barometric pressure at the aerodrome (called QFE) is set on the sub-scale, it indicates height above the aerodrome. If the sub-scale setting is changed so that the instrument on the ground at the aerodrome shows the elevation of the aerodrome above sea level, the pressure set on the sub-scale is called QNH. With QNH set, the instrument shows the aircraft's altitude above sea level in the vicinity of that aerodrome. In the UK, a 'regional QNH' or Regional Pressure Setting (RPS) is published as the lowest forecast QNH in the region (if used it will give extra separation from the ground, because the altimeter will always under-read). If the sub-scale is set to 1013 hectopascals (the Standard Pressure Setting or SPS), the instrument will show what is referred to as 'pressure altitude'.

The normal pressure setting for flight at low altitudes is QNH. In the UK, QFE is sometimes used for flight in the circuit pattern. SPS (1013 hPa) is used for cruising flight above a certain altitude (the Transition Altitude).

Transition altitude in the UK is generally 3000 feet, but higher in certain controlled airspace. When climbing above transition altitude, a pilot should set 1013 hPa on the subscale. Confusion between 'altitude' and 'pressure altitude' is avoided by referring to pressure altitudes in 'steps' of 100 feet called "flight levels". For example a pressure altitude of 4500 feet would be referred to as 'flight level 45', written as 'FL45'.

The pilot must reset his altimeter sub-scale to QNH before descending below transition altitude. Varying sea level pressures mean that the flight level corresponding to transition altitude changes from day to day, so the Met office publishes a 'transition level' which is the lowest flight level (in steps of 5) above transition altitude. Before descending through transition level, the pilot must set QNH (QFE is a practical alternative if entering a traffic pattern immediately). The gap between transition altitude and transition level is called the 'transition layer'.

5.10 Flight Plans

Flight plans must be 'filed' by most pilots wishing to fly in Controlled Airspace, and there is an ICAO format. However, there are other circumstances when such a flight plan is mandatory.

- IFR flight in Advisory Airspace (see Chapter 7)
- Flight across international borders (crossing the UK FIR boundary)
- Flight in areas as required by the appropriate ATS authority.

Pilots may submit a flight plan whenever they wish, and are encouraged to do so when flying over mountainous or sparsely populated areas or over the sea more than 40nm from the coast.

The contents of a flight plan include the departure point, destination, route and altitude, the flight rules to be followed, the time of departure, the speed and total time of flight, and alternate aerodromes at which the pilot may land if unable to land at his planned destination. For search and rescue purposes (see Chapter 10), it should also include the aircraft's endurance, the number of people on board, and any emergency equipment carried.

The flight plan should be submitted at least 60 minutes before departure, but the UK allows that to be reduced to 30 minutes for flights outside Controlled or Advisory Airspace. A delay of over an hour requires the cancellation of the original plan and the re-submission of an amended one. Flight plans can be filed in the air, and must be cancelled after landing.

5.11 Instrument Flight Rules Cruising Levels

If the pilot is unable or unwilling to comply with VFR, he must use his instruments to avoid collisions. Of course, he will ask ATC for assistance if it is available, but there are things he himself can and must do to reduce the risk of collisions. The basic rule is that all aircraft cruising (flying straight and level) must do so with their altimeters showing **complete thousands of feet** (or tens of flight levels), which naturally implies they must use the same altimeter datum of QNH below transition altitude and SPS above transition level. This implies that there can be no cruising under IFR in the transition layer.

If tracking to the **West**, the thousands must be divisible by 2 (**even** thousands); if tracking to the **East**, they must be **odd** thousands. The tracks are to be measured as **magnetic tracks**. Between 000° and 179° counts as Easterly, between 180° and 359° counts as Westerly. These are shown in figure 5.1 below and are often referred to as the 'semicircular rules'. Above FL290 certain levels are omitted, and the expression 'even' no longer applies literally to the levels available for westerly tracks. This is because of the inaccuracies of 'sensitive' altimeters at high level. Certain airspace is reserved for aircraft which carry modern accurate altimeter and autopilot systems, and in that '**RVSM**' (Reduced Vertical Separation Minima) airspace all the thousands of feet can be used, so the expressions Odd and Even apply literally there up to and including FL410. The semicircular rules give no protection if an aircraft is climbing or descending.

In the UK, the Semicircular rules only apply above FL245. Below FL245 we use a quadrantal system (FL245 itself is not used). Aircraft tracking between 000°(M) and 089°(M) fly at odd thousands of feet, those tracking between 090°M and 179°M cruise at odd thousands of feet plus 500 feet, (e.g. FL75) between 180°M and 269°M cruise at even thousands, and between 270°M and 359°M cruise at even thousands plus 500 feet, (e.g. FL65).

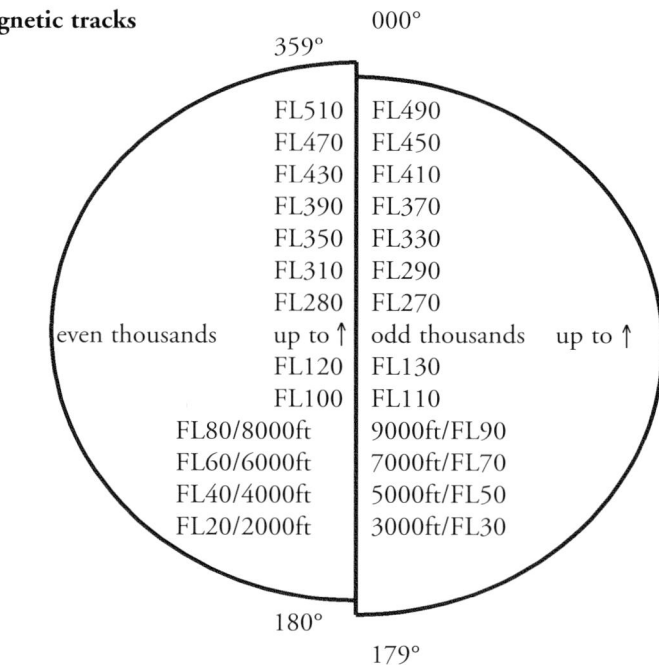

FIGURE 5.1 NORMAL IFR CRUISING ALTITUDES AND FLIGHT LEVELS

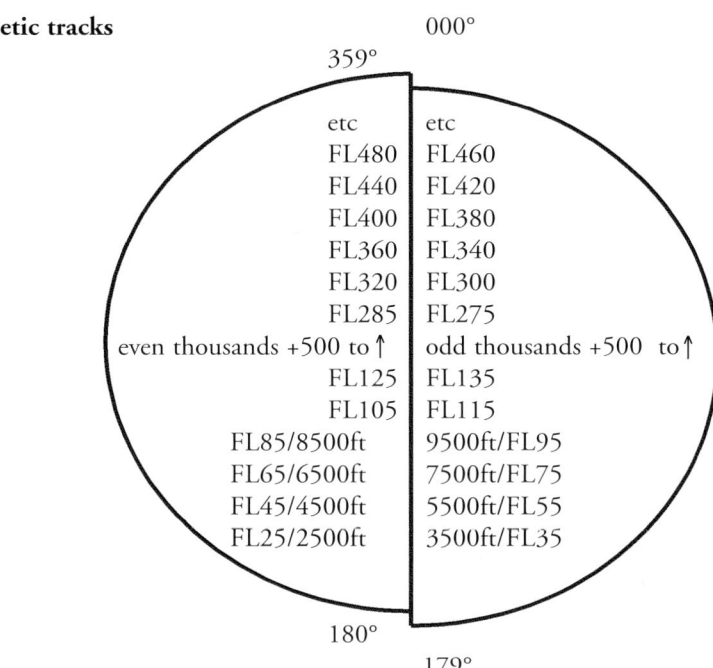

FIGURE 5.2 ICAO VFR CRUISING ALTITUDES AND FLIGHT LEVELS

5.12 IFR Minimum Altitude

The Instrument Flight Rules assume that the pilot is unable to see the ground or any obstructions. Therefore there are laid down minimum altitudes below which an IFR pilot may not fly at particular stages of flight. Annex 2 only lays down minimum levels for cruising (flying straight & level), and even these only apply if national authorities have not laid down their own. However, the **ICAO minima** are that aircraft must fly at least 1000 feet above the highest obstacle **within 8 km** of its estimated position, or **2000 feet** in **mountainous** terrain. Navigational accuracy should be taking into account when estimating position. This minimum altitude is in addition to the concurrent requirement to be able to make a safe landing away from congested areas and assemblies of people.

In the UK, the mountainous terrain rule does not apply. However, IFR aircraft are required to keep 1000 feet clearance above fixed objects within a distance of 5 nm (9.25 km), although that regulation does not apply to an aircraft following IFR at or below 3000 feet amsl if the aircraft is clear of cloud and in sight of the surface.

5.13 IFR Pre flight requirements

An aircraft wishing to fly under IFR must carry **suitable instruments** and **navigation equipment** appropriate to the route to be flown. A pilot wishing to carry out a flight under IFR must make a careful study of available current **weather reports and forecasts** and consider fuel requirements and **alternative courses of action** in case the flight cannot be completed as planned.

5.14 IFR in Controlled Airspace

Having looked at the basic rules, which apply in uncontrolled airspace, we can see that, without some other assistance, there is no guarantee of avoiding collisions in the open FIR. IFR merely reduce the risk. IFR give no help during changes in altitude or track. However, in most parts of the world, controlled airspace exists to provide additional safety. In order to fly under IFR in controlled airspace, a pilot requires an instrument (or in the UK Class D airspace an IMC) rating, which is outside the scope of this document.

5.15 Unlawful Interference

If an aircraft is being subjected to unlawful interference, commonly called "hijacking", the crew are to make every attempt to **inform ATC** of that fact, possibly by using the word 'hijack', by squawking mode A code 7500 on the SSR transponder, and /or using Data Link. They should also try to pass all relevant **information about the interference**, and certainly any **deviation** from the current flight plan, so that ATC can afford the aircraft priority.

5.16 Exercise

1. ICAO Annex 2 lists the Rules of the Air. Where do they apply?

    a. Over the high seas only
    b. Everywhere unless they conflict with the laws of the State being overflown
    c. Over the territory of signatory nations only
    d. Everywhere except in JAA States

2. An aeroplane in the UK is flying under VFR over a congested area of a town. What is the minimum height it may fly?

    a. 1500 feet above any fixed object within 2000 feet of it
    b. At a height which will enable it to land clear in the event of an engine failure
    c. It must comply with both (a) and (b)
    d. Neither (a) nor (b)

3. What is the minimum flight visibility for flight in VFR if an aircraft is flying at 5000 feet in Class G airspace at a speed of 120 knots and in sight of the surface?

    a. 8000 metres
    b. 5000 metres
    c. 1500 metres
    d. There is no minimum

4. What is the minimum horizontal distance which an aeroplane must stay away from cloud in Class D airspace at 2000 feet in order to fly under VFR?

    a. 1500 metres
    b. 1800 metres
    c. no minimum stated provided the aircraft has a flight visibility of 5000 metres
    d. no minimum stated provided the aircraft is in sight of the surface

5. What is the minimum flight visibility for an aeroplane to fly under VFR at 2500 feet in class A airspace?

    a. 8000 metres
    b. 5000 metres
    c. 1500 metres if clear of cloud and in sight of the surface
    d. VFR flight is not permitted

6. What is the maximum speed for an aircraft to fly under VFR at 8000 feet in class G airspace in the UK?

    a. 180 knots
    b. 250 knots
    c. 350 knots
    d. There is no limit

7. What is the minimum height above a congested area which a pilot may fly under Visual Flight Rules according to ICAO Annex 2?

    a. 1000 feet above the highest object within 600 metres of the aircraft
    b. 1000 feet above the highest object within 2000 metres of the aircraft
    c. 1500 feet above the highest object within 2000 feet of the aircraft
    d. 1500 feet above the highest object within 2000 metres of the aircraft

8. What is the minimum height outside congested areas at which ICAO standards permit normal flight to take place under VFR?

    a. 1000 feet above ground or objects, no minimum above water
    b. 1000 feet above ground or water
    c. 500 feet from any person, vessel, vehicle or structure, but no minimum height
    d. 500 feet above ground or water

9. The aircraft's heading is 175° true. Drift is 4° right. Variation is 3° west. Which of the following would be a correct altitude to cruise under VFR in Europe?

    a. any altitude would be correct
    b. 2500 feet
    c. 3500 feet
    d. 4000 feet

10. The aircraft's heading is 185° true. Drift is 4° left. Variation is 3° east. Which of the following would be a correct altitude to cruise under IFR in Europe?

   a. 2500 feet
   b. 3000 feet
   c. 3500 feet
   d. 4000 feet

11. The aircraft's heading is 175° true. Drift is 4° right. Variation is 3° west. Which of the following would be a correct altitude to cruise under IFR in the UK?

   a. 2500 feet
   b. 3000 feet
   c. 3500 feet
   d. 4000 feet

12. What is the minimum cruise altitude under IFR (over non-mountainous terrain) allowed by ICAO?

   a. 1000 feet above the highest fixed object within 600 metres of its position
   b. 1000 feet above the highest fixed object within 2000 metres of its position
   c. 1000 feet above the highest fixed object within 8 km of its position
   d. 1500 feet above the highest fixed object within 600 metres of its position

13. What mode A transponder setting means an aircraft is suffering unlawful interference?

   a. 7000
   b. 7500
   c. 7600
   d. 7700

14. What is the minimum flight visiblity for a PPL(A) holder with no additional ratings to fly as pilot-in-command under VFR in Class G airspace in the UK below 3000 feet?

   a. 1500 metres
   b. 1800 metres
   c. 3000 metres
   d. 5000 metres

INTENTIONALLY LEFT BLANK

Chapter 6

Signals & Definitions

6.1 Interception by Military Aircraft

a. Introduction

Interception of a civil aircraft by military aircraft is a dangerous affair. ICAO decrees that it should be used only as a last resort, and only for the purpose of **identification**, or for the **safe navigation** of the civil aircraft.

b. Action by the Intercepted Aircraft

For safety, the intercepted aircraft must immediately **obey all signals** given by the interceptor. The pilot should **inform ATC** of the interception, squawking mode A **code 7700**, and try to establish radio contact with the interceptor on **121.5 MHz** (and 243.0 MHz if carried). The message should include the identity of the intercepted aircraft and the **nature of its flight**. Treat any instructions given by the interceptor as top priority (after all, he has a gun!)

c. Signals from the Interceptor

He will signal that he has intercepted you and wants you to follow him by appearing in front of your (usually) **left side**, at the same level, and **rocking his wings**, then turning slowly left onto the direction he wants you to **follow**. At night he will also flash his **navigation lights**.

If he is satisfied that you may continue on your way, he will make a **rapid climbing turn** away from you (what the military call a 'break').

If he lowers his **landing gear** while you are still following him, he wants you to **land** at the airfield over which he is flying at the time. He will lead you above the runway he wants you to land on. At night he will also switch on his **landing lights**.

If you have informed him that you cannot comply with one of his instructions, (see below), he will perform the 'break', but only to tell you he **understands**. He will almost certainly come back and lead you somewhere else.

d. Signals to the Interceptor

When you see you have been intercepted, **rock your wings** to tell him you understand, and will follow him. At night, also flash your **navigation lights**. The same applies to tell him you understand that he has released you when he 'breaks'.

If he has told you to land, lowering your **gear** (and switching on your landing lights at night) tells him you will comply, but if the airfield is **not adequate**, tell him by **raising it** again over the runway at a height of between 1000 and 2000 feet, and continuing to circle. (At night you also flash your landing or other lights). If you **cannot comply** with his order to land, or any other order, tell him by switching your **lights on and off** in a **regular** fashion. Switching them in an irregular fashion means you are **in Distress!**

6.2 Signals from ATC

In the event of communications failure, ATC may use visual signals, by means of a lamp or pyrotechnics, to pass messages to aircraft. The colours have logical meanings. **Green** is a positive clearance (go), **Red** rejects the clearance (stop doing what you are trying to do). **Flashing** the lamps modifies the basic meaning of the light. **Flashing White** is an order for the aircraft to come to the ramp, stop and come to ATC. The light signals are shown below with their exact meanings to aircraft either on the ground or in the air. The aircraft receiving the signals should **acknowledge** them by **rocking its wings** (or moving its ailerons or rudder on the ground) by day, or **flashing** the landing (or navigation) lights **twice** at night. It is worth mentioning that one is not expected to rock one's wings on the final approach, or indeed on the base leg.

a. Signals to aircraft on the ground

i. **Flashing green** gives clearance to **taxi** to the holding point

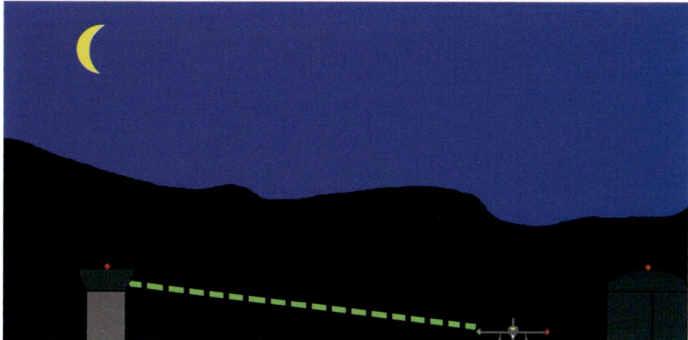

CLEAR TO TAXI

ii. **Steady green** gives clearance to **take-off**.

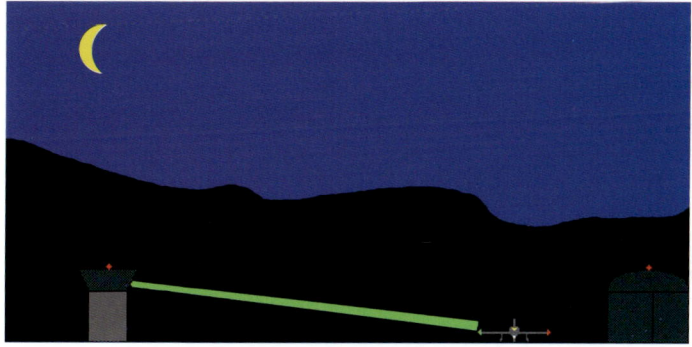

CLEAR TO TAKEOFF

iii. **Steady red** means stop in your present position.

STOP

iv. **Flashing red** is an order to taxi away from the landing area.

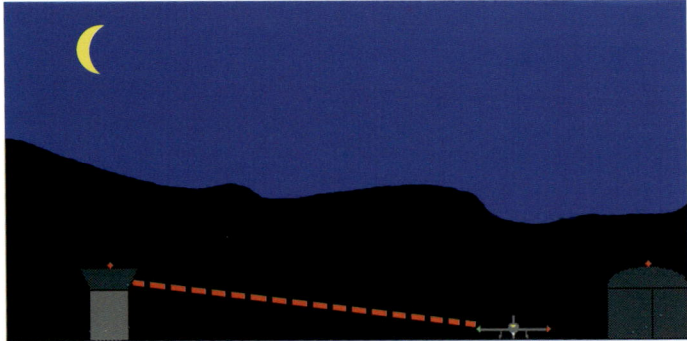

Taxi away from the landing area

v. **Flashing white** is a clearance, or in fact an order, to return to the apron (officially, your starting point on the aerodrome)

Return to the ramp

b. Signals to aircraft in the air

  i. **Steady green** is a clearance to land

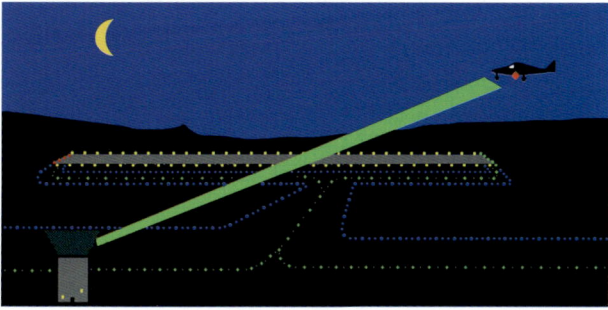

CLEAR TO LAND

  ii. **Steady red** means do not land from this approach - **go around**, (the actual words are to "give way to other aircraft and continue circling").

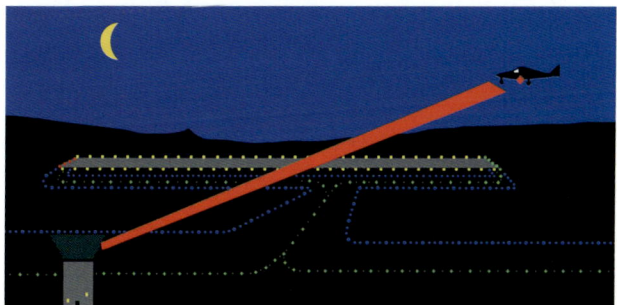

GO AROUND

  iii. **Flashing red** says the **aerodrome is unsafe** - the aircraft must divert.

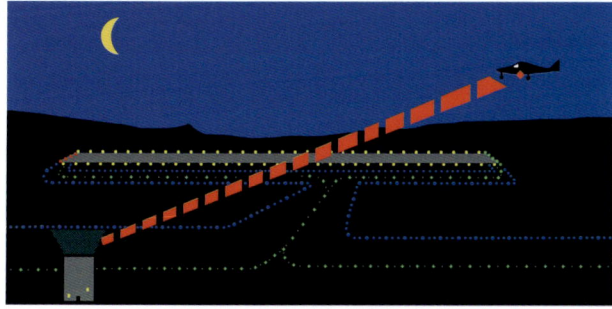

DO NOT LAND - DIVERT

iv. **Flashing green** means you may **enter the traffic pattern**, land after further clearance.

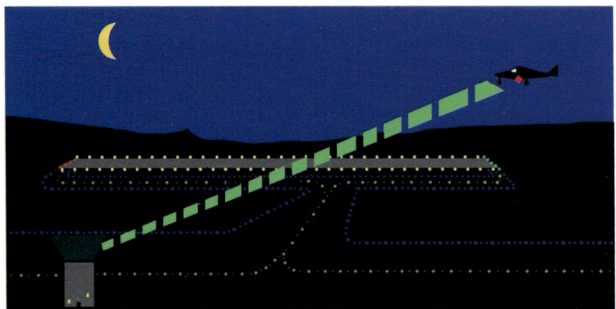

ENTER THE TRAFFIC PATTERN

v. **Flashing white** is an instruction to **land at this aerodrome** after receiving a steady green light, and taxi to the apron, again after receiving clearance.

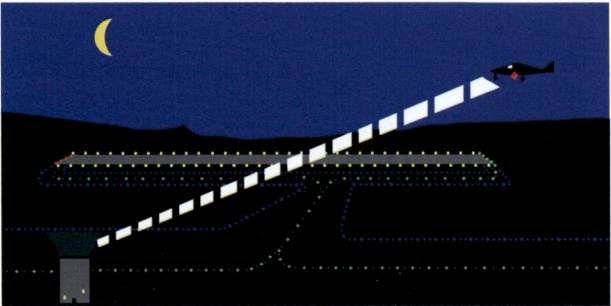

LAND AT THIS AIRFIELD

c. **Red pyrotechnics.**

The firing of a red pyrotechnic (flare) has a similar meaning to a steady red light to an aircraft in the air. It **cancels** any previous clearance to an aircraft on the final approach and instructs it to **go around immediately**.

6.3 Signals from an Aircraft

a. Distress Signals

We are no longer in the era of the Titanic. However, **SOS** still means "I am in distress", and these letters, or a morse message, over W/T or with lights, spelling them out (••• — — — •••), can still be used to mean "**Grave and imminent danger threatens, and I need immediate assistance**". However, most communications are made by radio now, or even data link, and the spoken or written word "**MAYDAY**" means the same. If other means fail, a succession of **red rockets** or red **starshells** conveys the message, as does a single red parachute **flare** fired from an aircraft.

b. Urgency Signals

If an aircraft is not actually in 'grave and imminent danger', there are still occasions when it is very important that someone acts quickly. Perhaps the danger is not 'imminent', but still 'grave', for example a fuel leak which prevents it reaching its destination. The pilot of such an aircraft will consider that he should pass that information to ATC urgently. He can use a special form of words to tell others that he has a very urgent message to transmit **concerning** the **safety** of a ship, aircraft, or other vehicle, or of some person on board or within sight. The words "**PAN PAN**", or the letters '**XXX**' should prefix the message. There may also be occasions when an aircraft has difficulties which require it to **land immediately**, but it does not require immediate assistance. In that case, if he cannot pass an urgency message to ATC by radio for some reason, the pilot should switch the **landing** lights and/or the **navigation lights** on and off **repeatedly**.

6.4 Marshalling Signals to an Aircraft

Aircraft are in their element when flying. However, on the ground they are less manoeuvrable, and it is often difficult for a pilot who is taxiing to see clearly whether all parts of his aircraft are clear of obstructions. On the apron, he will sometimes be given the services of a person on the ground to guide, or 'marshal' his aircraft safely into or out of a safe parking position. That 'marshaller' will often use **bats**, or **illuminated 'wands'** at night, and will use some of the signals detailed here. However, the pilot in command is still responsible for the safety of his aircraft.

a. General Instructions

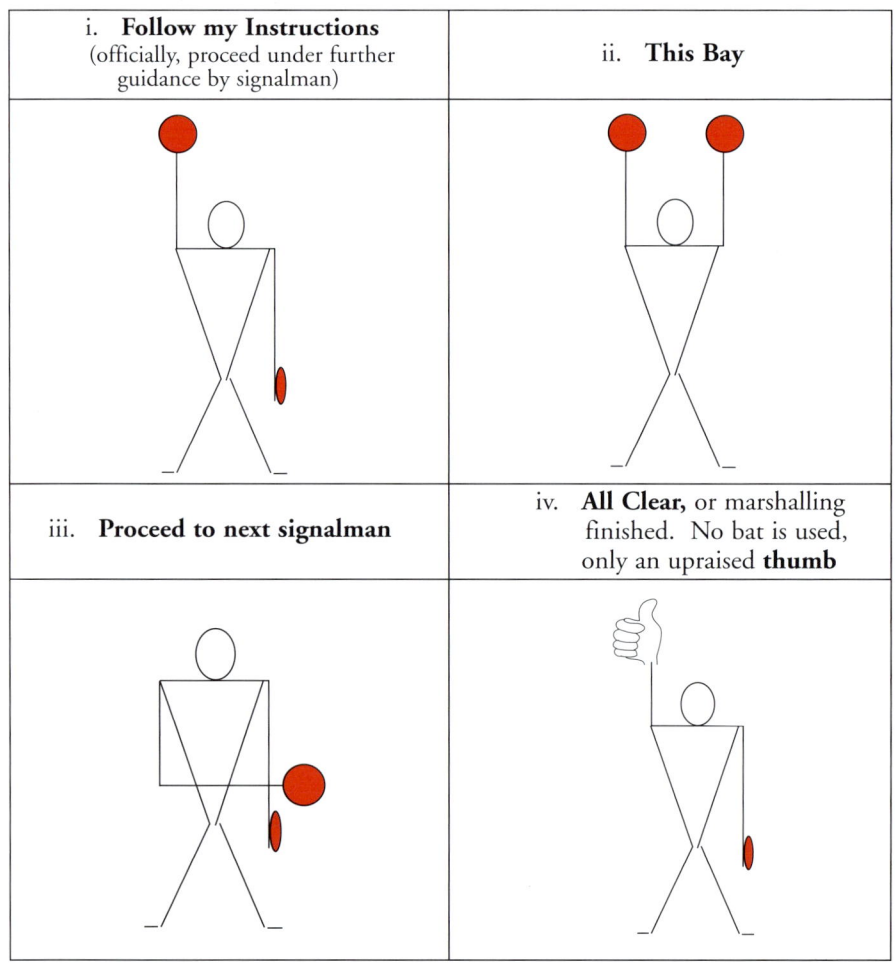

i. **Follow my Instructions** (officially, proceed under further guidance by signalman)	ii. **This Bay**
iii. **Proceed to next signalman**	iv. **All Clear,** or marshalling finished. No bat is used, only an upraised **thumb**

b. Moving Instructions

The signaller will move his arms and bats or wands as he wants the aircraft to move. The speed of arm movement indicates the **rate** at which he wants the pilot to move the aircraft. If the aircraft is to move **ahead**, he will make a **beckoning** movement with his palms towards himself, from waist level upwards. If to move **backwards**, he will make a pushing motion with his palms towards the aircraft from below to shoulder level. If a turn is required, he will point one hand, bat or wand downwards in the **direction of the wheel which he wants to slow down** or stop, while continuing to wave the other hand to encourage that wheel to continue as normal. To stop the aircraft, he will cross his arms above his head repeatedly. Again, the **rate** of crossing his arms indicates **how quickly** he wants the aircraft to stop.

i. **Move ahead**

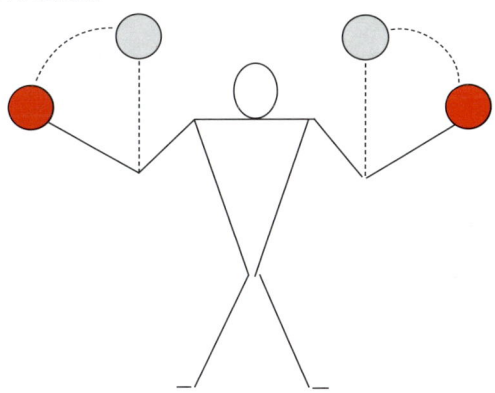

ii. **Stop**

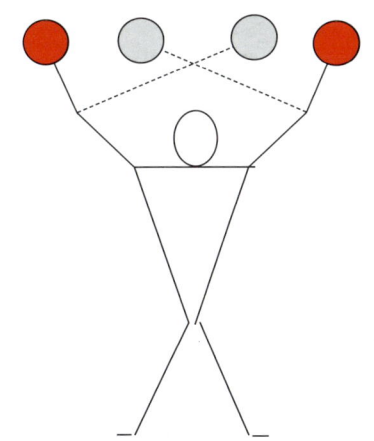

iii. **Turn Right** while moving **forward**.

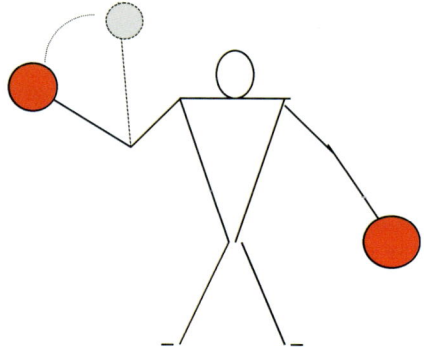

iv. **Turn Left** while moving **forward**.

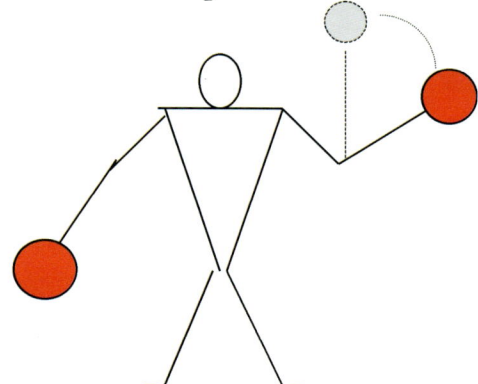

viii. **Slow down.** The signaller moves his arms in a flapping motion, palms, bat or wands **downwards**.

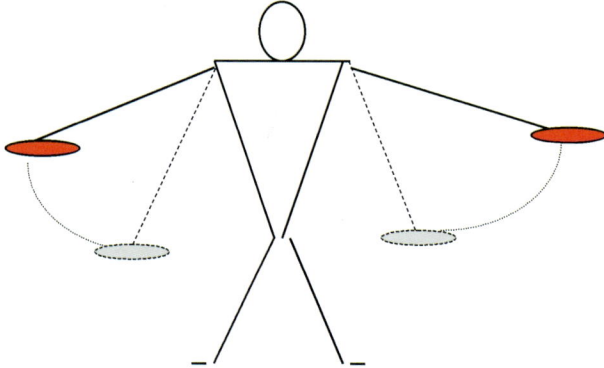

c. **Engine Controls**

  i. **Cut** (stop) **engines**.
  The signaller draws his flat hand, bat or wand across his throat as if cutting it.

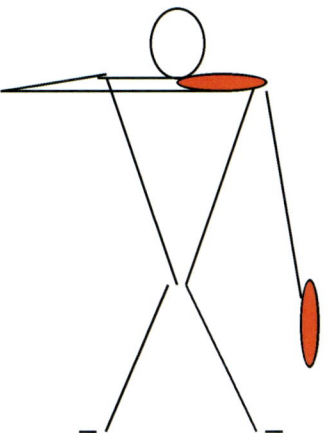

  ii. **Start number .... engine**.
  The signaller raises the number of **fingers** on his left hand corresponding to the number of the engine (measured from port outer towards the starboard) to be started, at the same time making a **circling** motion with his right hand.

iii. **Reduce power on the engine on the indicated side**. The signaller uses the slow down signal, but only on the side which he wants the power reduced on, in this case the left.

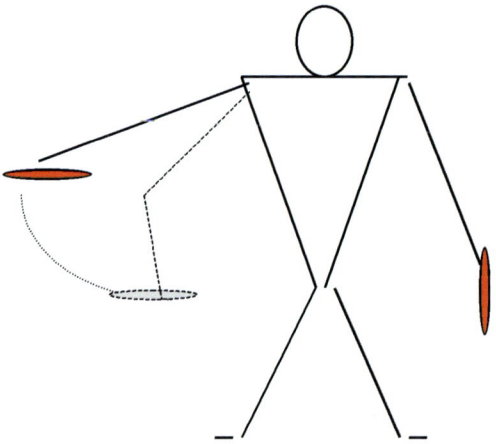

d. **Operation of Services.** The signaller may use these to either instruct the pilot to do something, or to indicate that something has been done, or to acknowledge a message from the pilot.

i. **Chocks inserted**. Often signalled with the thumbs pointing inwards and the palms toward the signaller.

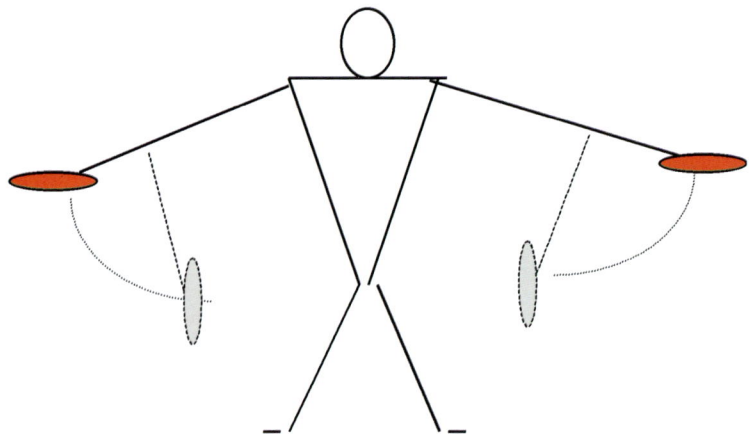

ii. **Chocks removed**. Often signalled with the thumbs pointing outwards and the palms toward the signaller.

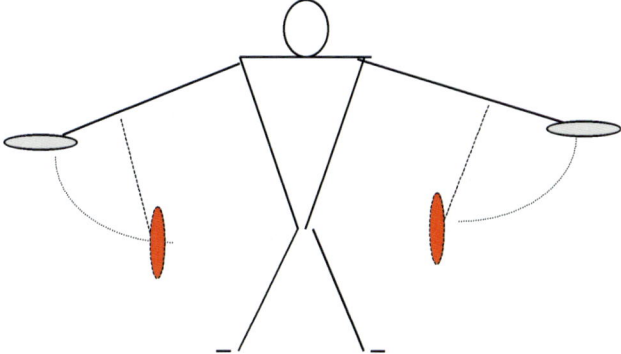

iv. **Engage brakes** (put them ON). He places his open hand in front of his body then makes a fist with the fingers.

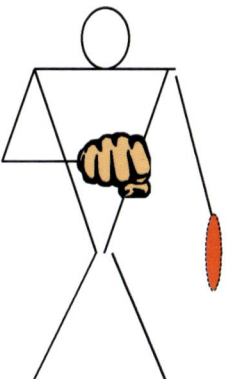

v. **Release brakes** (let them OFF). He places his fist in front of his body then opens his hand.

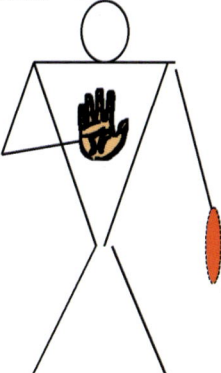

6.5 Marshalling Signals from the Pilot

If the pilot wishes to make signals to the marshaller, he must ensure his hands are clearly visible to the marshaller, and use the following.

a. **Brakes engaged**.
Raise his open hand in front of his face, then clench the fist at the moment of applying brakes.

b. **Brakes released**.
Raise his clenched fist in front of his face, then open his hand at the moment of releasing the brakes.

c. **Insert Chocks**.
With open hands, he should start with his arms as extended as possible, then cross his open hands in front of his face.

d. **Remove Chocks** Starting with open hands crossed in front of his face, extend his arms as far as possible, keeping the hands open.

e. **Ready to start number ..... engine**.
The engine again is numbered from port outer towards the starboard. The pilot raises his hand with the corresponding number of fingers extended. The example indicates number 2 engine.

6.6 Ground Signals for General Information

Information about an aerodrome can be given out in various ways. One way is for ATC to place certain markings on the ground which can be seen by aircraft overhead who may wish to join the traffic pattern. Annex 2 lays down the meaning of some of these markings.

a. Manoeuvring Area.

The manoeuvring area is defined as *that part of the aerodrome used for takeoff, landing and taxiing.* It does not actually include aprons, which are defined as *areas set aside to accommodate aircraft for the purposes of loading, unloading, parking, and maintenance.* Signals affecting the use and condition of the manoeuvring area include:

i. A **white or yellow cross** on the ground indicates an **area unfit** for the movement of aircraft.

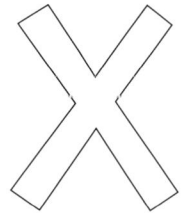

ii. A **white dumbbell** displayed in a signal area indicates that all takeoffs landings and taxiing must be **confined to runways and taxiways** respectively (these may be soft surfaces but must be marked).

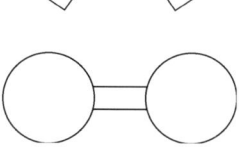

iii. The same dumbbell with **black bars** across the ends indicates that, although **takeoffs and landings must be confined** to runways, it is safe to taxi outside the marked taxiway

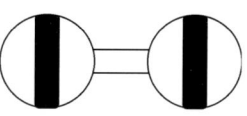

b. Traffic Pattern

Signals affecting flight around the traffic pattern include the following:

i. A **red square** in the signals area affects landings. If it has a **yellow diagonal**, it means that **special precautions** must be taken during the approach and landing.

ii. The same red square with a **yellow cross** tells pilots that **landings are prohibited**, probably for a long time.

iii. A **white or orange T** in the signals area indicates the **direction** of landing, parallel to the long arm and towards the cross piece. (i.e. to left in the picture). A circle of the same colour above the 'T', as shown, indicates that take-offs may not be in the same direction.

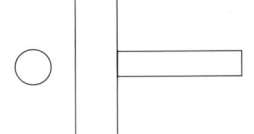

iv. A set of **2 digits** displayed vertically at or near the control tower indicates the actual **runway number** (in tens of degrees) to aircraft and persons on the ground.

27

v. An **arrow pointing to the right**, displayed either in the signal area or at the end of the runway in use, indicates that the traffic **pattern is right hand**. (officially that all turns after takeoff and before landing should be to the right).

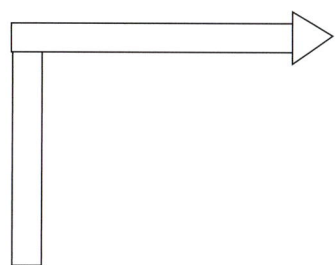

vi. A **double white cross** in the signal area indicates that **glider flying** is taking place from the aerodrome.

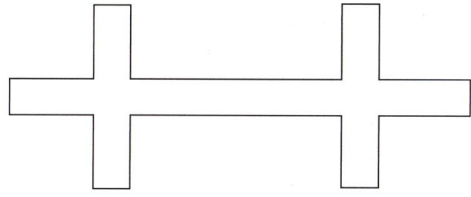

c. **Air Traffic Control**
A further sign depicts the place where pilots are to **report** when required. It is a black letter C on a yellow background.

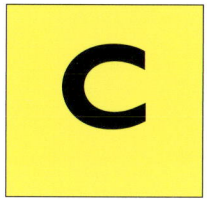

6.7 Definitions

Some definitions have been given in previous paragraphs in the last three chapters, and where they are exact definitions as in Annex 2, they are written in italics. However, many other words are defined in the Annex. Some are self-explanatory, others are not. You must be able to recognise and distinguish them from each other. Some are given here, others later, and some will be repeated.

Definitions of Vehicles, Places and People

AIRCRAFT
Any machine that can derive support in the atmosphere from the reactions of the air other than the reaction of the air against the earth's surface.

AEROPLANE
*A **power-driven heavier-than-air aircraft**, deriving its lift in flight chiefly from aerodynamic reactions on surfaces which remain fixed under given conditions of flight.*

FLYING MACHINE
A power-driven heavier than air aircraft. *(UK definition)*

AERODROME
A defined area on land or water (including any buildings, installations and equipment) intended to be used either wholly or in part for the arrival, departure and surface movement of aircraft.

MOVEMENT AREA
That part of an aerodrome to be used for take-off, landing, and taxiing of aircraft, consisting of the manoeuvring area and apron(s).

MANOEUVRING AREA
That part of an aerodrome to be used for the takeoff, landing, and taxiing of aircraft, excluding aprons.

APRON
A defined area on a land aerodrome, intended to accommodate aircraft for purposes of loading or unloading passengers, mail or cargo, fuelling, parking or maintenance.

AIRCRAFT STAND
A designated area on an apron intended to be used for the parking of aircraft.

Landing Area
That part of a movement area intended for the landing **or take-off** of aircraft.

Runway
A defined rectangular area on a land aerodrome **prepared** for the landing and taking-off of aircraft.

Taxiing
Movement of an aircraft on the surface of an aerodrome under its own power, excluding take-off and landing.

Taxiway
A defined path on a land aerodrome established for the taxiing of aircraft and intended to provide a link between one part of the aerodrome and another.

Signal Area
An area on the aerodrome used for the display of ground signals.

Air Traffic
All aircraft in flight or operating on the manoeuvring area of an aerodrome.

Aerodrome Traffic
All traffic **on** the manoeuvring area of an aerodrome and all aircraft flying **in the vicinity** of an aerodrome.

Controlled Aerodrome
An aerodrome at which air traffic control service is provided to aerodrome traffic.

Safety Sensitive Personnel
Persons who might endanger aviation safety if they perform their duties and functions **improperly**, including, but not limited to, crew members, aircraft maintenance personnel and air traffic controllers.

Flight Crew Member
A licensed crew member charged with duties **essential** to the operation of an aircraft during flight time.

Pilot in Command
The pilot responsible for the operation and safety of the aircraft during flight time.

Definitions of Positions and Directions

LEVEL
A generic term relating to the vertical position of an aircraft in flight and meaning variously height, altitude, or flight level.

Note: A pressure type altimeter when calibrated in accordance with the Standard Atmosphere will indicate altitude when set to a QNH altimeter setting, will indicate height above the QFE reference datum when set to a QFE altimeter setting, and may be used to indicate flight levels when set to a pressure of 1013.2 hPa.

ALTITUDE
The vertical distance of a level, a point, or an object considered as a point, measured from **mean sea level**. (Since maps indicate elevation above mean sea level, altitudes can be compared with map elevations to ensure safe clearance above obstructions.)

HEIGHT
The vertical distance of a level, a point, or an object considered as a point measured from a **specified datum.**

PRESSURE-ALTITUDE
An atmospheric pressure expressed in terms of altitude which corresponds to that pressure in the **Standard Atmosphere**. Standard Atmosphere is defined elsewhere.

FLIGHT LEVEL
A surface of constant atmospheric pressure which is related to a specific pressure datum, **1013.2** *hectopascals (hPa) and is separated from other such surfaces by specific pressure intervals.*

TRANSITION ALTITUDE
The altitude at or below which the vertical position of an aircraft is controlled by reference to **altitudes.** (Below transition altitude, pilots must have QNH set on their altimeters.)

CRUISING LEVEL
A level maintained during a significant portion of a flight.

HEADING
The direction in which the longitudinal axis of an aircraft is **pointed**, *usually expressed in degrees from North (true, magnetic, compass or grid).*

Track
The projection on the earth's surface of the **path** of an aircraft, the direction of which path at any point is usually expressed in degrees from North (true, magnetic, compass or grid).

Reporting Point
A specified geographical location in relation to which the position of the aircraft can be reported.

Ceiling
The height above ground or water of the **base of** the lowest layer of **cloud** below 6000 metres (20,000 feet) covering more than half the sky.

Visibility
The ability, as determined by atmospheric conditions and expressed in units of distance, to **see and identify** prominent unlighted objects by day and prominent lighted objects by night.

Ground Visibility
The visibility at an aerodrome, as reported by an accredited observer.

Flight Visibility
The visibility **forward from the cockpit** of an aircraft in flight.

Visual Meteorological Conditions
Meteorological conditions expressed in terms of visibility, distance from cloud, and ceiling equal to or better than specified minima. The specified minima are at para 5.4

VMC
The symbol used to designate visual meteorological conditions.

Instrument Meteorological Conditions
Meteorological conditions expressed in terms of visibility, distance from cloud, and ceiling, less than the minima specified for visual meteorological conditions. (If conditions are worse than VMC, they are IMC)

IMC
The symbol used to designate instrument meteorological conditions.

Extra Bits

PSYCHOACTIVE SUBSTANCES
Alcohol, opioids, cannabinoids, sedatives and hypnotics, cocaine, other psychostimulants, hallucinogens, and volatile solvents, whereas coffee and tobacco are excluded. (Drugs and booze)

PROBLEMATIC USE OF SUBSTANCES
*The **use** of one or more psychoactive substances by aviation personnel in a way that:*

   a. *constitutes a direct **hazard** to the user or endangers the lives, health or welfare of others; and /or*
   b. *causes or worsens an occupational, social, mental, or physical **problem** or disorder.*

6.8 The Reason for the Definitions of Extra Bits

Annex 2 actually lays down that anyone defined as '**safety-sensitive personnel**', in other words those who could endanger aviation safety if they do not do their job properly, must not try to carry out their function while **under the influence** of any psychoactive substance (drugs or booze), which impairs performance. Such safety sensitive personnel are also forbidden to engage in any kind of '**problematic use of substances**' (See definitions above).

6.9 Exercise

1. If a military aeroplane flies alongside you and rocks its wings, what should you do?

    a. Follow it
    b. Call on 121.50 MHz
    c. Select 7700 on your transponder
    d. All the above

2. What does a steady red light from ATC indicate to the pilot of an aircraft in flight?

    a. Go-around
    b. Do not land, divert
    c. Land at this aerodrome after receiving a green light
    d. Give way to other aircraft and continue circling

3. What does a flashing white light from ATC indicate to the pilot of a taxiing aircraft?

    a. Clear the landing area immediately
    b. Taxi to the holding point for the runway in use
    c. Hold your position and await a flashing green light
    d. Return to the starting point on the aerodrome

4. What light signal indicates to the pilot of an aircraft in the air that he may land?

    a. A steady green light
    b. A flashing green light
    c. Both (a) and (b)
    d. Neither (a) nor (b)

5. If a marshaller holds his left hand down and waves his right arm continually upwards and backwards, what does he want the pilot to do?

    a. Turn right while moving forward
    b. Turn left while moving forward
    c. Start the left engine
    d. Start the right engine

6. What signal should the pilot use to tell his ground handler that his brakes are on?

   a. Show his open hand then close it
   b. Show his closed hand then open it
   c. Cross his hands in front of his face
   d. Place his crossed hands in front of his face then uncross them

7. What does a white dumbell in the signal area mean?

   a. Landing prohibited
   b. Take-offs, landings and taxiing must be made on paved surfaces only
   c. Take-offs and landings must be made on paved surfaces, taxiing may be on grass
   d. Make all take-offs, landings and taxiing on marked surfaces, which may be grass

8. What ground signal indicates the runway in use to an aircraft in the air?

   a. A white T in the signal area
   b. White numbers in the signal area
   c. Either (a) or (b)
   d. Neither (a) nor (b)

9. In the signals area there is a red square with a yellow diagonal. What does this mean?

   a. The traffic pattern is right hand
   b. All turns after take-off and before landing must be to the right
   c. Landing prohibited
   d. Take special care during approach and landing

10. What is defined as *"Any machine that can derive support in the atmosphere from the reactions of the air other than the reaction of the air against the earth's surface"*?

   a. An aircraft
   b. A flying machine
   c. An airship
   d. An aeroplane

11. What is defined as *"The vertical distance of a level, a point, or an object considered as a point, measured from mean sea level"*?

   a. Height
   b. Altitude
   c. Flight Level
   d. All three can be defined in this way

Chapter 7

Airspace

7.1 Introduction

Although the Chicago Convention allows aircraft to fly over every state's territory, the safety of air navigation requires certain restrictions to be placed on such flight. For this reason, the airspace above ICAO Contracting States and the High Seas is divided in certain ways. One division is into 'restricted' and 'unrestricted' airspace, dictating where aircraft may fly. Another division relates to the amount of control that the state places on the flight.

7.2 Restricted Airspace

Restricted airspace, from which aircraft are normally excluded unless specifically permitted or in an emergency, is listed in the Aeronautical Information Publication (AIP) for each state. It is normally divided into categories defining the particular restriction. The three categories in use in the UK are:

- Danger Areas   (marked on a chart as D with a number)
- Prohibited Areas   (marked as P with a number)
- Restricted Areas   (marked as R with a number)

Restricted Airspace may only be restricted at certain times, in which case details are listed in the AIP. The AIP lists all Restricted Airspace with its individual number and its dimensions. Charts show Restricted Airspace outlined in red and marked with its descriptive letter and serial number (eg R313).

7.3 Danger Areas

A Danger Area is defined as airspace where activities dangerous to the flight of an aircraft take place. These may be military firing ranges, explosive factories, or anything else which poses a danger. Flight in such areas is often not prohibited, although there may be statutory instruments or bye laws which affect the land and the airspace above it. However, the ANO makes it an offence to endanger an aircraft or any person, and flying through a Danger Area would normally be considered endangering one's aircraft.

In the UK, Danger Areas have allocated responsible Air Traffic Service Units, which can give pilots information as to the status of the area (Danger Area Information Service). A few may be able to provide a Danger Area Crossing Service (DACS). However, unless specifically told that a Danger Area is inactive, pilots must assume it is active, and avoid it for safety.

7.4 Prohibited Areas

Prohibited Areas are just that. Flight inside such airspace is prohibited. In the UK there are very few Prohibited Areas.

7.5 Restricted Areas

Restricted Airspace which is neither a Danger Area nor a Prohibited Area is described simply as a Restricted Area. They are effectively prohibited areas, but certain aircraft may fly in them if they comply with specific regulations. These are all listed in the AIP. In the UK, several Restricted Areas apply only to helicopters.

7.6 Controlled Airspace

a. Types of Controlled Airspace

Like a road on the surface, airspace which becomes busy requires an element of control over the traffic inside it to allow it to flow smoothly and safely. Such airspace is called 'Controlled Airspace'. Airspace in which no control is provided is 'uncontrolled airspace'. Different types of Controlled Airspace are given different names. The definitions here are simplified from the official ones.

Controlled Airspace touching the ground, surrounding one or more aerodromes, is called a 'Control Zone' (CTZ). There is actually a minimum size for a CTZ; ICAO lays down that it must include airspace out to at least 5 nm from the centre of the aerodrome along the runway approach.

Controlled Airspace which does not touch the ground, usually surrounding a Control Zone, is called a 'Control Area' (CTA), and depending on its purpose may be referred to as a 'Terminal Manoeuvring Area (TMA)'. A Control Area in the form of a corridor between two or more CTAs or CTZs is called an 'Airway', and may be regarded as a highway in the sky. Airways are a minimum of 10 nm wide, but may be wider in certain areas.

b. Airspace Classification

Airspace over the world is classified according to the amount of control which Air Traffic is deemed to require. The classification is one of a series of letters, alphabetically decreasing in control from A to G. Basically, in Class A airspace, pilots must always obey the Instrument Flight Rules, which in Controlled Airspace are quite stringent, although in the UK flight under 'Special VFR' is sometimes permitted. As the classification decreases towards G so the amount of control decreases.

For practical purposes, Classes A to E are regarded as 'Controlled Airspace'. Class F, in which Air Traffic Control is only given to those aircraft operating under IFR and requesting it, is 'Advisory Airspace', and together with Classes A to E is described as Air Traffic Services Airspace, but because there is no requirement for any aircraft to be controlled, it is not Controlled Airspace. Class G is of course neither controlled nor subject to Air Traffic advice, although certain services are available on request.

In the UK, Class A airspace, mainly airways but also some CTZs, is out of bounds to private pilots without an instrument rating unless they can obtain Special VFR clearance. Class B airspace is above Flight Level 245, and all aircraft there are provided with ATC separation from each other. There is no Class C airspace at the time of writing in the UK, but in class C airspace, ATC gives all aircraft which are following the Instrument Flight Rules (IFR) positive separation from all traffic (IFR or VFR) in the airspace.

In Class D airspace, ATC only provides separation to IFR traffic from other IFR traffic. However, all VFR traffic must obtain ATC clearance to enter Class D airspace. Pilots must therefore ensure that ATC knows all about their flight, and obey all ATC instructions even though they are flying under the Visual Flight Rules (VFR). In Class E airspace, ATC provides the same IFR from IFR separation as in Class D, but VFR traffic does not need to give ATC any information provided they maintain the Visual Fight Rules in controlled airspace (see chapter 5).

The AIP lists all Controlled and Advisory Airspace in a country's airspace, and the ATC units which control them, together with the radio frequencies for initial contact with them. It also lists any special rules which pilots must obey in them.

7.7 Aerodrome Traffic Zone

An Aerodrome Traffic Zone (ATZ) surrounds most aerodromes. It has the same classification as the airspace around it. An ATZ includes all airspace from the ground to 2000 feet above airfield elevation, out to a radius of 2 nautical miles from the centre of the longest runway, or 2.5 nm if the runway is 1850 metres or longer. Even in Class G airspace, aircraft must not enter an ATZ during the aerodrome's published opening hours without the permission of the owner, and unless they comply with the traffic pattern. In fact, legally they must comply with the traffic pattern in the vicinity of any aerodrome.

Aerodromes may be controlled by an Air Traffic controller, in which case his permission is needed to take-off or land or to move on the manoeuvring area. If there is no Air Traffic Control, there may be a flight information service available from a Flight Information Service Officer (FISO), whose permission is required for ground movement, including entering the runway, but not for any flying clearances. Smaller aerodromes may only have a communications service given by an air/ground operator, who cannot give any instructions or permission, and can only give information if specifically asked.

7.8 Military Air Traffic Zones

In the UK, Military Air Traffic Zones (MATZ) surround most military aerodromes. A MATZ normally has dimensions from ground level to 3000 above airfield elevation out to 5 nm radius from the centre of the longest runway. There is also usually at least one extension or 'stub' along the main instrument runway out to 10 nm, from 1000 feet to 3000 feet above airfield elevation. Civil aircraft are not legally required to recognise a MATZ, but safety reasons make it advisable to inform ATC of their position when approaching a MATZ (ideally 10 miles or 5 minutes before), and to conform with ATC requests inside one.

7.9 Air Traffic Services

Air Traffic Services are provided to help pilots. They attempt to prevent collisions between aircraft in the air and on the manoeuvring area, and to maintain an orderly flow of air traffic. They also provide advice and information for the safe and efficient conduct of flights, and notify and assist the SAR organisation (see Chapter 10) if an aircraft requires their aid.

Outside Controlled Airspace in the UK, a Flight Information Service is available on published radio frequencies from FISOs at Air Traffic Control Centres. They can provide altimeter setting information, and weather and aerodrome status reports if requested. They can accept a flight plan. They are also able to accept and pass on 'Airep Specials', which are reports from aircraft in flight about severe weather conditions which they have experienced. In addition, they provide an Alerting Service for the emergency services in the event of an accident or airborne emergency to any aircraft which they know about.

Other Air Traffic Controllers may be able to provide more comprehensive assistance to pilots. There are Lower Airspace Radar Service (LARS) units operated from various aerodromes around the country. Many aerodromes offer a radar Approach Control Service to arriving or departing 'controlled flights'. In both of these, Radar Information Service (RIS) may be available if the ATC unit has the spare capacity. Under RIS, in addition to the FIS, a controller will pass information about traffic which he can see on his radar set and which is close to the aircraft to which he is giving the service. It is up to the pilot to decide on any avoiding action which may be needed.

Radar Advisory Service (RAS) is more comprehensive, and again may be available if the ATC unit has the spare capacity. Under RAS, the controller will not only pass information as in RIS above, but will advise the pilot what to do. He will give 'vectors' (directions to fly) to avoid the conflicting traffic. The controller will attempt to keep the aircraft separated by 5 miles or more (or a certain distance vertically depending on what he knows about the confliction). Because avoiding action may take the aircraft into cloud, a pilot not qualified to fly in IMC should accept a RAS **only if he can follow ATC vectors and still maintain VMC**. If the pilot does not wish to take the advice of the controller, he must tell him and accept that the service is now a RIS instead. In fact, in the UK at the time of writing, RAS is only given if the pilot is following Instrument Flight Rules.

Because both RIS and RAS require the controller to have spare capacity, a pilot who has asked for a particular service must not assume he is getting it. The service is only in force after a 'contract' has been made and accepted between controller and pilot. In other words, both the pilot and the controller have actually agreed what standard of service is being given. Instructions from the controller to assist in identifying the aircraft are not a radar service. Once the controller is happy he can safely offer the service to the pilot he will say "G-xxxx Radar Advisory", or "G-xxxx Radar Information". That is the moment the service starts.

Radar Control is given by controllers in controlled airspace. A pilot must obey ATC instructions if he is under radar control unless they would lead to an unsafe situation or a breach of the law. If a pilot cannot obey ATC instructions, he must request an amended clearance.

Flight in controlled airspace may be allowed under 'procedural control'. This involves an air traffic controller giving instructions without the use of radar, and normally involves asking the pilot to make position reports at regular intervals. Some 'Special VFR' flights may be conducted under procedural control.

7.10 Secondary Surveillance Radar

A radar controller will often use 'secondary' radar when providing a service. The SSR transponder fitted to many light aircraft assists him in this. A 'transponding' aircraft will show clearly on his radar screen, indicating the code which the pilot has selected on his control unit. If the transponding aircraft has the altitude reporting facility (called Mode C or mode Charlie) selected, the controller will also see the aircraft's pressure altitude displayed on his screen.

If the controller is providing a service to the aircraft, he will ask the pilot to 'squawk' a particular code. However, any aircraft not under his control. and not squawking will not show on his screen so well, or in some cases at all. Pilots not receiving a radar service are therefore requested to select code '7000' on mode A of their transponder at all times with mode C when fitted.

Codes 7700, 7600, and 7500 indicate various forms of emergency. When selecting a code on the transponder, pilots are advised to switch their transponder to 'standby' before changing the code, and then reselect mode A, and C if available, after the new code has been selected.

Airliners are progressively being equipped with airborne collision avoidance systems (ACAS). These systems receive the signals from another aircraft's transponder and warn the crew of its position. If the received SSR signal contains an altitude message, they will also calculate and indicate safe avoiding action.

7.11 Distress and Diversion

In the UK, a unique service is provided by the Air Traffic Control Centres. A team of controllers continuously monitors the emergency radio frequency 121.5 MHz. If they hear a call on that frequency, or the military emergency one of 243 MHz, they have a direction finding facility which gives bearings to the transmitter from many stations around the country. In the South East of the country, they have an 'auto-triangulation' facility which produces a series of lines on a chart automatically, and the controller can fix the position of the transmitter. They also watch radar screens for an emergency squawk.

Unfortunately, the service relies on line-of-sight communications. Aircraft which are low may have their transmissions blanked by hills, so only limited fixing may be available. However, the controllers will do their best to guide an aircraft with a problem away from danger and provide all assistance possible to avoid accidents. Assistance may have to be prioritised, and Distress calls ('Mayday') have top priority, and Urgency calls (Pan Pan) come second (see chapter 9). However, navigation assistance can be provided if no higher priority call is being dealt with, and pilots may practise the use of the service by using the call prefix 'Practice Pan'.

7.12 Definitions

Division of Airspace

AIR TRAFFIC SERVICE (ATS)
A generic term meaning variously, flight information service, alerting service, air traffic advisory service, and air traffic control service.

AIR TRAFFIC SERVICES AIRSPACE
Airspaces of defined dimensions, alphabetically designated, within which specific types of flights may operate and for which air traffic services and rules of operation are specified. ATS airspaces are **classified** as Class A to G.

CONTROLLED AIRSPACE
An airspace of defined dimensions within which air traffic control service is provided to IFR flights and to VFR flights in accordance with the airspace classification. Controlled Airspace is a generic term which covers airspace classes **A, B, C, D and E.**

CONTROL ZONE
A controlled airspace extending upwards from the surface of the earth to a specified upper limit. ('Zone comes up from Zero')

CONTROL AREA
A controlled airspace extending upwards from a specified limit above the earth. ('Area comes up from the Air')

AIRWAY
A control area or portion thereof established in the form of a **corridor**.

TERMINAL CONTROL AREA
A control area normally established at the confluence of ATS routes in the vicinity of one or more major aerodromes. (Usually where airways traffic wants to descend into major aerodromes)

AIR TRAFFIC CONTROL SERVICE
A service provided for the purpose of **preventing collisions** *between aircraft, and between aircraft and obstructions on the manoeuvring area, and for expediting and maintaining an orderly flow of traffic.*

Aerodrome Traffic Zone
An airspace of defined dimensions established around an aerodrome for the protection of aerodrome traffic.

Advisory Airspace
An airspace of defined dimensions, or designated route, within which air traffic advisory service is available.

Advisory Route
A designated route along which air traffic advisory service is available.

Air Traffic Advisory Service
A service provided within advisory airspace to ensure separation, in so far as is practical, between aircraft which are operating on IFR flight plans.

Flight Information Region
An airspace of defined dimensions within which flight information and alerting service are provided.

Flight Information Service
A service provided for the purpose of giving advice and information useful for the safe and efficient conduct of flights.

Alerting Service
A service provided to notify appropriate organisations regarding aircraft in need of search and rescue aid, and to assist such organisations as required.

Danger Area
An airspace of defined dimensions within which activities dangerous to the flight of aircraft may exist at specified times.

Restricted Area
An airspace of defined dimensions, above the land area or territorial waters of a State, within which the flight of aircraft is restricted in accordance with certain specified conditions.

Prohibited Area
An airspace of defined dimensions, above the land area or territorial waters of a State, within which the flight of aircraft is prohibited.

Aeronautical Information Publication (AIP)
A publication issued by or with the authority of a State and containing aeronautical information of a lasting character essential to air navigation. (In the AIP, pilots will find information about controlled and advisory airspace, as well as Restricted Areas, Prohibited Areas and Danger Areas).

Air Traffic Services

Air Traffic Services Unit
A generic term meaning variously, air traffic control unit, flight information centre, or air traffic services reporting office.

Air Traffic Control Unit
A generic term meaning variously, area control centre, approach control office, or aerodrome control tower.

Area Control Centre
A unit established to provide air traffic control service to controlled flights in control areas under its jurisdiction.

Area Control Service
Air Traffic Control service for controlled flights in control areas.

Approach Control Office
A unit established to provide air traffic control service to controlled flights **arriving at, or departing from**, one or more aerodromes.

Approach Control Service
Air traffic control service for **arriving or departing** controlled flights.

Aerodrome Control Tower
A unit established to provide air traffic control service to aerodrome traffic.

Aerodrome Control Service
Air traffic control service for aerodrome traffic.

Controlled Flight
Any flight which is subject to an air traffic control clearance.

AIR TRAFFIC CONTROL CLEARANCE (often shortened to '**Clearance**')
Authorisation for an aircraft to proceed under conditions specified by an air traffic control unit.

FLIGHT INFORMATION CENTRE
A unit established to provide flight information and alerting service.

AERONAUTICAL STATION
A land station in the aeronautical mobile service. In certain instances, an aeronautical station may be located, for example, on board ship or on a platform at sea. (A radio station)

APPROPRIATE ATS AUTHORITY
The relevant authority designated by the State responsible for providing air traffic services in the airspace concerned.

APPROPRIATE AUTHORITY
a. <u>*Regarding flight over the **high seas*** -</u>
*The relevant authority of the **State of registration.***
b. <u>*Regarding flight other than over the high seas* -</u>
*The relevant authority of the State having **sovereignty** over the territory being overflown.*

Flight Procedures

FLIGHT PLAN
Specified information provided to air traffic services units, relative to an intended flight or portion of flight of an aircraft.

ATS ROUTE
A specified route designed for channelling the flow of traffic as necessary for the provision of air traffic services. 'ATS route' includes airways, advisory routes, controlled or uncontrolled routes, arrival and departure routes, etc. An ATS route is defined by a route designator, significant points and the track and distance between them, reporting requirements and often the lowest safe altitude as determined by the appropriate ATS authority.

VFR *The symbol used to designate the visual flight rules.*

VFR Flight *A flight conducted in accordance with the visual flight rules.*

Special VFR Flight
*A VFR flight cleared by air traffic control to operate **within a control zone** in meteorological conditions **below** VMC.*

IFR *The symbol used to designate the instrument flight rules.*

IFR Flight *A flight conducted in accordance with the instrument flight rules.*

Radiotelephony
A form of radiocommunication primarily intended for the exchange of information in the form of speech. (As distinct from 'wireless telegraphy' or 'W/T' which was used to describe communication by morse code.)

Traffic Information
*Information issued by an air traffic services unit to **alert** a pilot to other known or observed air traffic which may be in proximity to the position or intended route of flight and to help the pilot avoid a collision.*

Traffic Avoidance Advice
*Advice provided by an air traffic services unit specifying **manoeuvres** to assist a pilot to avoid a collision.*

Airborne Collision Avoidance System (ACAS)
*An aircraft system based on secondary surveillance radar (SSR) transponder signals which operates **independently** of ground-based equipment to provide advice to the pilot on potential conflicting aircraft that are **equipped with** SSR transponders.*

Estimated Time of Arrival
*For VFR flights, the time at which it is estimated that the aircraft will arrive over the **aerodrome*** (Estimated time overhead) (Note - 'estimated time of arrival' (ETA) only applies to arriving at destination. Estimates for reporting points are just that, 'estimates' and not ETAs).

TOTAL ESTIMATED ELAPSED TIME
*For VFR flights, the estimated time required from take-off to arrive over the destination **aerodrome**.* (Total time from take-off to overhead)

ALTERNATE AERODROME
*An aerodrome to which an aircraft may proceed when it becomes either **impossible** or **inadvisable** to proceed to or to land at the aerodrome of intended landing. Alternate aerodromes include the following:*

TAKE-OFF ALTERNATE
An alternate aerodrome at which an aircraft can land should this become necessary shortly after take-off and it is not possible to use the aerodrome of departure.

EN-ROUTE ALTERNATE
An aerodrome at which an aircraft would be able to land after experiencing an abnormal or emergency condition while enroute.

DESTINATION ALTERNATE
An alternate aerodrome to which an aircraft may proceed should it become either impossible or inadvisable to land at the aerodrome of intended landing. (Almost the same as the general definition)

Modern Technology

DATA LINK COMMUNICATIONS
A form of communication intended for the exchange of messages via a data link. (Voice communication is unnecessary)

AUTOMATIC DEPENDENT SURVEILLANCE (ADS)
A surveillance technique in which aircraft automatically provide, via a data link, data derived from on-board navigation and position-fixing systems, including aircraft identification, four-dimensional position and additional data as appropriate. (The pilot need not even press a button!)

INTENTIONALLY LEFT BLANK

7.13 Exercise

1. Which type of controlled airspace touches the ground?

   a. A Terminal Control Area
   b. An Airway
   c. A Control Zone
   d. A Restricted Area

2. What colour would the boundary of a Restricted Area be marked on a chart?

   a. Red
   b. Blue
   c. Green
   d. Yellow

3. What Air Traffic Service gives a pilot information about possible conflicting traffic but no advice as to the correct action to take to avoid it?

   a. Radar Advisory Service
   b. Radar Information Service
   c. Radar Control
   d. Flight Information Service

4. Which of the following air traffic services require the pilot to obey ATC instructions if he is receiving the service?

   a. Radar Control & Radar Advisory Service
   b. Radar Control only
   c. Radar Advisory Service & Radar Information Service
   d. Radar Control & Procedural Control

5. Whose permission must a pilot obtain before moving his aircraft on the manoeuvring area?

   a. An Air Traffic Controller only
   b. A FISO or an Air Traffic Controller only
   c. An air/ground operator, a FISO, or an Air Traffic Controller
   d. No-one's permission is required unless the aircraft enters the runway

6. What are the (i) horizontal and (ii) vertical dimensions of the aerodrome traffic zone of an aerodrome whose longest runway is 1000 metres long?

   a. (i) 2 nm radius from the centre of that runway   (ii) up to 2000 feet agl
   b. (i) 2½ nm radius from the centre of that runway   (ii) up to 2000 feet agl
   c. (i) 2½ nm radius from the centre of the airfield (ii) up to 3000 feet agl
   d. (i) 2 nm radius from the centre of the airfield   (ii) up to 2000 feet agl

7. Which of the following airspace classes are controlled airspace?

   a. A, B, C only
   b. A, B, C, D only
   c. A, B, C, D, E only
   d. A, B, C, D, E, F only

8. In which Class of controlled airspace does ATC provide separation to IFR traffic from all other traffic, no separation between VFR traffic, but VFR traffic must have clearance to enter the airspace?

   a. Class B
   b. Class C
   c. Class D
   d. Class E

9. ATC may provide an Approach Control Service. For what traffic is it primarily provided?

   a. All aircraft arriving at the aerodrome only
   b. All aircraft arriving or departing the aerodrome
   c. Controlled traffic arriving at the aerodrome only
   d. Controlled traffic arriving or departing the aerodrome only

10. What is defined as *"A service provided within advisory airspace to ensure separation, in so far as is practical, between aircraft which are operating on IFR flight plans."*?

    a. Air Traffic Control Service
    b. Air Traffic Advisory Service
    c. Flight Information Service
    d. Air Traffic Alerting Service

11. The definition of a "reporting point" is " a specified geographical location ....."

    a. at which the position of the aircraft must be reported?
    b. in relation to which the position of the aircraft must be reported?
    c. at which the position of the aircraft can be reported?
    d. in relation to which the position of the aircraft can be reported?

12. What is defined as *"A unit established to provide flight information and alerting service"*?

    a. Air Traffic Service Unit
    b. Aeronautical Service
    c. Area Control Service
    d. Flight Information Centre

13. In which class of airspace does ATC provide separation for IFR traffic from all other IFR traffic, but relies on VFR traffic to provide its own separation from all other traffic?

    a. Class B
    b. Class C
    c. Class D
    d. Class E

INTENTIONALLY LEFT BLANK

Chapter 8

The Aerodrome

8.1 Introduction

Aerodromes for international civil air traffic use are set out in accordance with ICAO Annex 14 volume 1. Heliports are in volume 2, but this guide is only concerned with airports for fixed wing aircraft.

In order to be licensed for flying training, or public transport, UK aerodromes must comply with similar rules. Any notable UK differences are listed in italics.

Aerodromes are given a **reference code** to show the kind of aircraft they are intended to serve. That code is then used to decide the facilities (and their characteristics such as size or number) necessary for the safe operation of these aircraft. The first part of the code deals with the length of runway required (the **reference field length**) by the intended aircraft, and is given by a number of which 1 is the shortest and 4 the longest. The second part is a letter, which defines the larger of wingspan or wheel track (called outer wheel span). The letters increase from A to E. An aerodrome for 747s would therefore be coded 4E, one for Cessna 150s coded 1A. Annex 14 lays down standards and recommended practices for each of the code combinations.

Aerodromes are divided into various parts. The **Movement Area** is the part which is used for the take-off, landing and taxiing of aircraft. It consists of runways and taxiways (which together form the Manoeuvring Area) and aprons.

An Apron is **a defined area, on a land aerodrome, intended to accommodate aircraft for purposes of loading or unloading passengers, mail or cargo, fuelling, parking or maintenance**. In other words, it is a parking area, although the ICAO name for a parking place is 'aircraft stand'.

A Taxiway is defined at paragraph 8.17, but in essence it is a path between the runway and apron.

8.2 The Runway

A Runway is a **defined rectangular area prepared for the landing and taking-off of aircraft**. The surface may be hard or natural. The whole of that area is not always available for both of these functions; parts of it may be unusable for safe landing because of obstructions close to the end, and obstructions at the other end may limit the length available for safe take-off. There will also be unprepared or semi-prepared surfaces available at the side and either end which may be usable with varying degrees of safety in an emergency but which are not safe for regular use. The parts of the runway and additional areas available for various uses are defined in Annex 14. Every aerodrome used for international civil air traffic publishes the length of the completely safe usable areas as **declared distances**, which are described below.

a. Landing

There is a basic **Landing Distance Available (LDA)**, which is the total length of runway less any part at the approach end which is unsafe because of obstructions or other reasons. The start of the LDA is the **threshold**, and if it is not also the start of the runway it is called a **displaced threshold**. Beyond the runway itself, there may be an area available in which an aircraft may be brought to a stop in an emergency, but which is not available for normal use; this is called the **stopway**. Fig 8.1 shows a runway with a displaced threshold and a stopway.

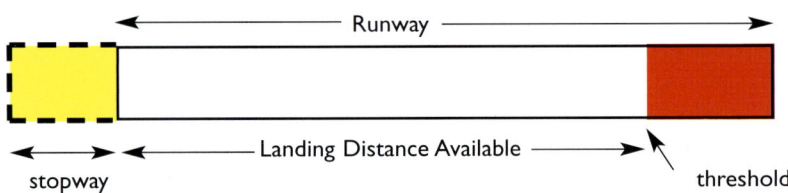

FIG 8.1 LANDING DISTANCE

b. Take-off

There is usually no reason why an aircraft should not start its take-off run at the beginning of the runway, and roll its wheels along the complete length and then climb away. The length declared for this is called the **Take-Off Run Available (TORA)** At the end of the TORA, there may be an area which is not suitable for an aircraft's wheels to roll on, but which is cleared of all obstructions. An aircraft taking off may **fly level** just above that area and accelerate to a safe climbing speed. That area is called a **clearway**, and in our figure it includes the Stopway, although that is not always the case. The **TORA plus the clearway** is declared as the **Take-Off Distance Available (TODA)**. If an aircraft has an emergency during its take-off roll, the pilot may decide to abandon the take-off and stop the aircraft. In that case, the stopway (if any) may be used to bring the aircraft to a halt. This total distance of **TORA plus stopway** is declared as the **Accelerate Stop Distance Available (ASDA)**. Fig 8.2 shows the same runway as before but as declared for takeoff.

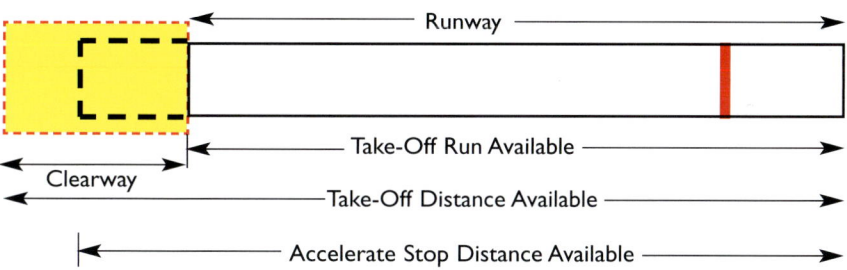

FIG 8.2 TAKEOFF DISTANCES

8.3 Runway Surface

The declared distances are used by pilots to decide whether they can land, take-off, or abandon a take-off safely. Other factors affect the performance of an aircraft when assessing that safety, such as slope, wind, and air density. A major factor affecting the ability of an aircraft to use its brakes efficiently, however, is the friction available between its tyres and the runway surface. Most runway surfaces give consistent braking under normal circumstances, and the characteristics of such surfaces are laid down in the ICAO Aerodrome Design Manual. However, water on the surface will considerably affect the efficiency of brakes, and so water in any form on the runway surface should be reported to the crew of an aircraft.

a. Liquid Water

A runway is reported as **DAMP** if the surface shows a change of colour due to water (ie becomes darker).

A runway is reported as **WET** if the surface is soaked, but there is no standing water.

It is reported as having **WATER PATCHES** if significant patches of standing water are visible.

It is reported as **FLOODED** when extensive standing water is visible.

Water patches or flooded runways are regarded as "contaminated" for purposes of performance calculations. If there are particular reasons why a runway may become slippery when wet, that fact should be reported to aircraft also, as it should if measurements show friction is low.

b. Frozen Water

In most cases, if water freezes, it gives even less friction to help the brakes than if the water is liquid. Such frozen, or partly frozen, water can be called **SNOW**, (either dry, wet, or compacted depending on the specific gravity) or **SLUSH**. Liquid water which has frozen in situ is **ICE**, and that is almost impossible to take-off or land on.

c. Reporting of Surface Condition

Aeronautical Information Service (AIS) and Air Traffic Services (ATS) units provide airfield information. That includes the following, most of which directly affect aircraft performance:

i) water on a runway, taxiway or apron

ii) snow, slush, or ice on a runway, taxiway or apron

iii) snow banks or drifts adjacent to a runway, taxiway or apron

iv) anti-icing or de-icing liquid chemicals on a runway or taxiway

v) rough or broken surfaces on a runway, taxiway or apron

vi) construction or maintenance work

vii) other temporary hazards, including parked aircraft

viii) failure or irregular operation of part or all of the aerodrome visual aids

ix) failure of the normal or secondary power supply

8.4 Construction Characteristics

a. Runway Strip

The Runway strip is a defined area including the runway and stopway, if provided, intended to reduce the risk of damage to an aircraft running off the runway, and to protect aircraft flying over it during take-off and landing operations. (Basically it is a flat area which can bear an aircraft's weight for a short time). It extends at least 30 metres before the threshold and beyond the end of the runway or stopway, and at least 75 metres each side of the centre line (low codes have larger strips). The edge where the runway surface itself merges with the rest of the strip must be flush, and the strip should be graded for the wheels of an aircraft running off the edge or end of the runway out to a distance of at least 40 metres (effectively about half the width of the strip). Figure 8.3 shows a typical runway strip.

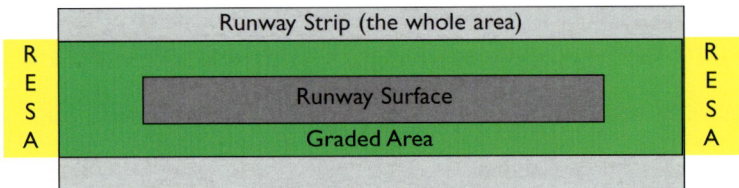

Fig 8.3 Runway strip and RESAs

b. Runway End Safety Area (RESA)

This is **an area symmetrical about the extended runway centre line and adjacent to the end of the strip primarily intended to reduce the risk of damage to an aeroplane undershooting or overrunning the runway.** It is provided on all instrument runways and on non-instrument runways on code 3 or 4 aerodromes. It extends at least 90 metres beyond the runway strip, and is at least twice the width of the runway surface. It may be soft enough to allow an aircraft to sink into it. RESAs are also shown in figure 8.3.

c. Clearway

A clearway is **defined as a defined rectangular area on the ground or water under the control of the Appropriate Authority, selected or prepared as a suitable area over which an aeroplane may make a portion of its initial climb to a specified height.** As shown in figure 8.2, it starts at the end of the takeoff run available, and should not be longer than half the TORA. It should extend to at least 75 metres either side of the extended run way centre line. 'Clearway' just means there are no obstacles to hit an aircraft with an engine failure while it tries to accelerate and start its climb.

d. Stopway

A stopway is **a defined rectangular area on the ground at the end of the take-off run available prepared as a suitable area in which an aircraft can be stopped in the case of an abandoned take-off.** If a stopway is provided (as in fig 8.1), it should be the same width as the runway.

e. Radio Altimeter Operating Area

Radio altimeters are used for automatic landings and approaches, so there are radio altimeter operating areas, where the ground does not change its elevation rapidly, before thresholds.

f. Taxiways

Taxiways should be wide enough for the aircraft they are designed to carry. However, basic width is not enough. As shown in figure 8.4, if a pilot follows the taxiway centre line with his nose wheel, the main wheels do not follow that centreline, but tend to cut the corner. To stop this corner cutting and possibly running the inboard wheels onto the grass, taxiways are **widened on the inside of bends.**

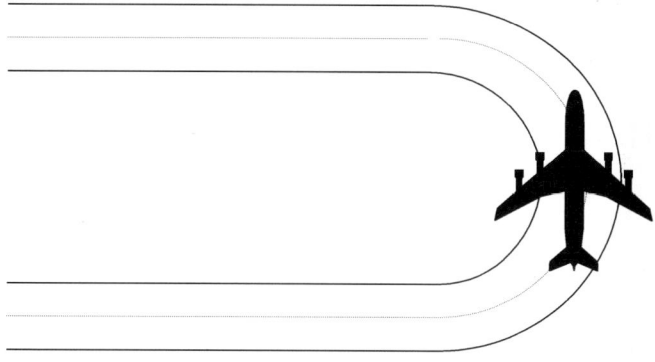

FIG 8.4 TAXIWAY BENDS

g. Holding Bays

A holding bay, used on some busy aerodromes, is rather like a lay-by on a major road.

h. Taxi-holding Position

Often called a 'holding point', this is a designated position at which taxiing aircraft and vehicles shall stop and hold position, unless otherwise authorised by the aerodrome control tower. These are established at an intersection of a taxiway with a runway, far enough away from the runway to give adequate clearance. In the case of precision approach runways, they must not interfere with the operation of radio aids.

j. Road-holding Position

A designated position at which vehicles may be required to hold on a road, like a taxi-holding position on a taxiway.

8.5 Visual Aids on Aerodromes

To reduce radio calls to a minimum, and to cater for the event of the failure of radio communication, various visual marks and signalling devices are used, in which case the meaning must correspond to the ones listed in Annexes 2 or 14 and given here.

Signalling Lamps

Every control tower has a lamp for making the signals in chapter 6, which can be pointed manually in any direction and should be able to signal in any of 3 colours - red, green and white. The colours can be rapidly changed, and the lamp should be able to send morse code in any of the colours.

Signal Area

Many of the ground signals listed in Annex 2 (Rules of the Air) and shown in chapter 6 can be conveniently placed in a specific signal area. That signal area must be an even horizontal surface at least 9 metres square, visible from 10° above the horizon from circuit height, and contrasting in colour from its signals with a white surround.

Wind Direction Indicators

One of these 'windsocks' must be visible from the air and from the manoeuvring area. It must be free from airflow disturbances caused by nearby objects, and be preferably orange or white as appropriate for contrast from its background, although other colours or combinations may be used. One should be marked with a white circle around it, and one should be illuminated at night.

Landing Direction Indicators

The T indicating the landing direction, as in figure 8.5, should be in a conspicuous place on the aerodrome, and be either white or orange to give maximum contrast with the background. It must be lit at night.

FIG 8.5 LANDING DIRECTION INDICATOR

8.6 Surface Markings

Markings painted on runways are **white**; those on taxiways and aircraft stands are **yellow**. Apron safety lines are in a conspicuous colour which contrasts with the aircraft stand markings (i.e. is not yellow!).

Runway Designator

A runway designation marking is painted at the threshold of a runway as a 2 digit number. This is the whole number nearest the one-tenth of the magnetic direction when viewed from the approach. If there is more than one parallel runway, the letters L, R, and if necessary C are used to show the left, right and centre runways. If there are more than 3 parallel runways, they are numbered in sets with one group numbered as the nearest tenth and the other as the next nearest tenth, and again designated as L, R or C.

Runway Markings

A runway is marked with a broken line along its length, down the centre line. The threshold is marked with lengthwise stripes or bars painted across the runway, as in figure 8.6. A displaced threshold is marked with a line across the runway followed by the stripes, with arrows in the unusable section if the displacement is permanent. The runway designator may sometimes be painted inside the threshold stripes, and on non-instrument runways of category 1 or 2 aerodromes, the threshold stripes or bars are not necessary. Side stripes as in figure 8.6 may be painted along the edges of the runway if the colour of the runway has poor contrast with its surroundings, and should be painted on all instrument runways. An aiming point mark in the form of a thick pair of parallel bars arranged as in figure 8.6 will be painted on the runway surface of code 2, 3 or 4 instrument runways between 150m and 450m from the threshold, depending on the LDA. Touchdown zone (TDZ) markings are provided on most precision approach runways, in the form of either pairs of parallel lines as in figure 8.6, or with a decreasing number of lines away from the threshold (i.e. 4 bars for the first mark, 3 for the second etc).

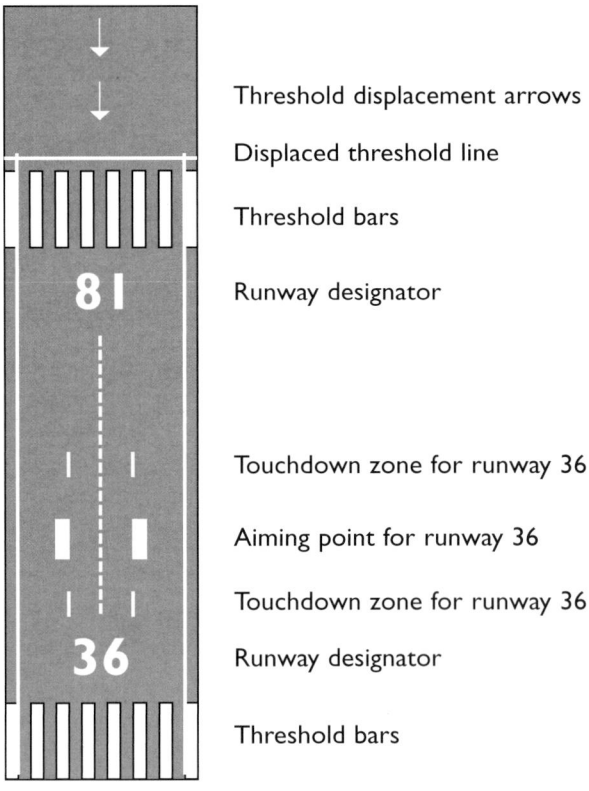

FIG 8.6-RUNWAY MARKINGS

Taxiway Markings

The centrelines of taxiways are usually marked with broken yellow lines from the runway to the stand markings on the apron. They follow the outside of bends, and curve onto the runway centreline where the taxiway serves as an exit. A broken line across the taxiway just before an intersection indicates that traffic must obtain clearance to cross it.

Taxi-Holding Position Markings

These indicate places where aircraft must hold and await clearance to enter the runway in use. The marking is a pair of unbroken yellow lines across the taxiway, followed by a pair of broken lines, as figure 8.7(a). When category II or III instrument approaches are in use, aircraft close to the runway may interfere with guidance signals, and holding positions further from the runway may be necessary. Yellow markings in the shape of a narrow grid across the taxiway, as figure 8.7 (b) indicate the holding position during such category II or III operations.

FIG 8.7 TAXI HOLDING POSITION MARKINGS

Aircraft Stand Markings

The only ICAO standard markings on an apron are the apron safety lines. These designate areas for the parking of ground equipment which allow safe separation from aircraft. They should be continuous, and of a colour which contrasts with the yellow of lines guiding aircraft (often red). They may include wingtip clearance lines and service road boundary lines. Other aircraft stand markings, in yellow, are to guide aircraft into and out of parking spaces with a safe clearance from obstructions. They will usually be marked with numbers or letters to assist the pilot.

Road Holding Position Markings

Ordinary road 'stop' markings are placed at all road entrances to a runway.

Information Marking

These are words, letters or numerals painted on the surface to supplement signs. They will be yellow (perhaps on black) for location information, and black (perhaps on yellow) for direction information.

8.7 Airfield and Runway Lighting

Aerodrome Beacon

An aerodrome beacon is sometimes placed at an aerodrome operating during the hours of darkness, unless the aerodrome is easily identifiable. It will show a flashing light of either white or green alternating with white. (Water aerodromes show a different colour). A separate identification beacon flashing a green light in a morse identification code may also be located on the aerodrome.

Runway Edge Lights

Runways with precision approach aids or intended for use by night have white lights spaced along their edge along their full length. Where there is a displaced threshold, the lights before that displaced threshold show red towards the approach. Lights on the edge of the last 600 metres (or last third of the runway) may be yellow. These and other lights are shown in figure 8.8.

Runway End Lights

A line of red lights across the runway mark the end of the runway whenever runway edge lights are provided. They show red towards an aircraft which is landing or taking off. See figure 8.8.

Runway Threshold Lights

A line of green lights across the runway marks the threshold of the runway, whether it is at the start of the runway or displaced, as in fig 8.8. A line of green lights on both sides of that line (wing bars) may provided extra conspicuity.

Runway Centreline Lights

The centreline of most instrument runways is marked by white lights. As the end of the runway approaches, the centreline lights change to red for the last 300 metres, and to alternating red and white for the 600 metres preceding that. (On short runways, the lights from two thirds of the runway length to the 300 metre mark alternate red and white). See figure 8.8.

Runway Touchdown Zone Lights

These barrettes (small groups of lights arranged across the runway) may be positioned alongside the edge lighting for up to the first half of the runway. Some of these lights are shown in figure 8.10.

Stopway Lights

If a stopway is available for use at night, red lights line the edge and the end of that stopway, as in figure 8.8.

Practical Considerations

All lights (including approach lights) which are obstacles (may be hit by an aircraft), must be of low mass and frangible (easily destroyed without damaging the aircraft).

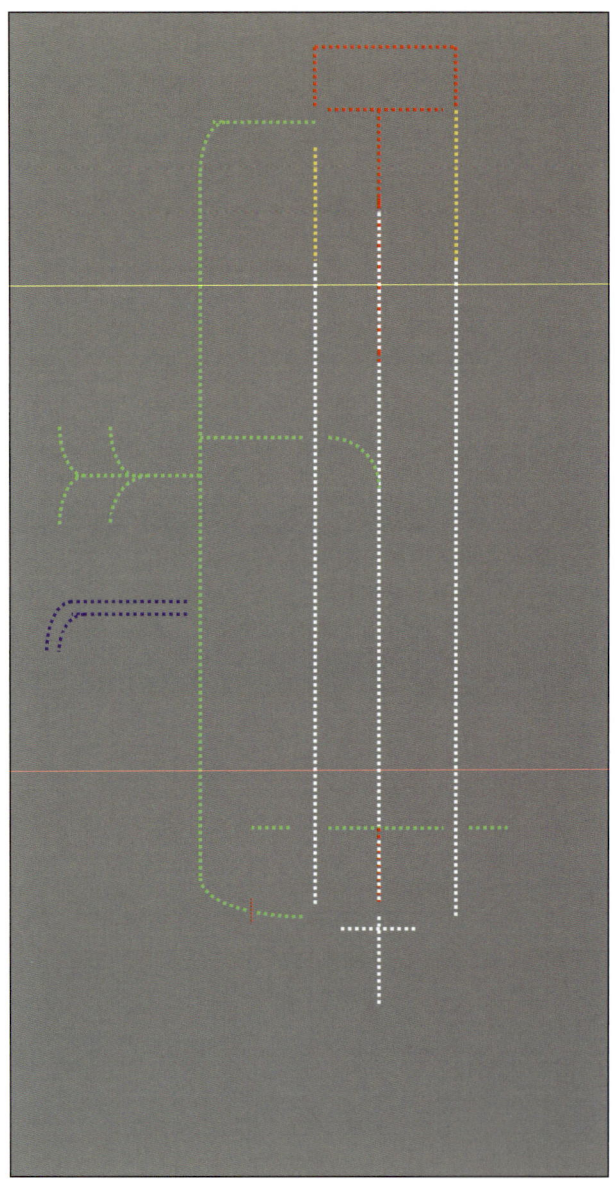

Fig 8.8 Movement area & simple approach lights

8.8 Taxiway and Apron Lights

Taxiway Centreline Lights
Green lights indicate the centre of a taxiway. They may also be used on a runway to indicate an exit route from the runway centreline to the taxiway, as shown on figure 8.8.

Taxiway Edge Lights
Where taxiway centreline lights are not provided, or on aprons, **blue** lights are placed at the edge of the taxiway. A short taxiway is marked like this in figure 8.8.

Stop Bars
Unidirectional **red** lights placed across the taxiway facing approaching traffic are provided at holding positions or taxiway intersections. These can be switched off by the air traffic controller when there is no need to stop. At taxi-holding positions, these stop bars are augmented by pairs of **alternating yellow** lights at the side of the taxiway. A stopbar is shown in figure 8.8 but would normally be only faintly visible from the air.

Runway Guard Lights
Sometimes on large airfields flashing yellow lights mark the entrance to every runway.

Road Holding Position Lights
Either red and green traffic lights, or flashing red lights, mark the road-holding position as if on a public highway.

8.9 Approach Lights

There are basically 3 types of approach lighting; simple, precision approach runway category I, and precision approach runway category II and III. Simple approach lighting is designed to guide pilots during non-precision approaches at night and in poor visibility by day.

Simple Approach Lighting

This consists of a row of lights extending from the threshold of the runway towards the approach along the extended centreline of the runway with a crossbar 300 metres from the threshold. There may be a further crossbar 150 metres from the threshold. There is no specific requirement as to colour of the lights, except that they should be readily distinguishable from other lights. A simple approach light system is part of figure 8.8.

Precision Approach Runway Category I

This system uses white lights to form a centreline extending to 900 metres from the threshold, again with a crossbar. Usually, centreline lights are doubled from 300 to 600 metres, and trebled from 600 to 900 metres, with further crossbars at 150 metre intervals. Alternatively, barrettes of lights may form the system, and these will normally be supplemented by capacitor discharge lights (strobes) flashing to guide the pilot towards the runway.

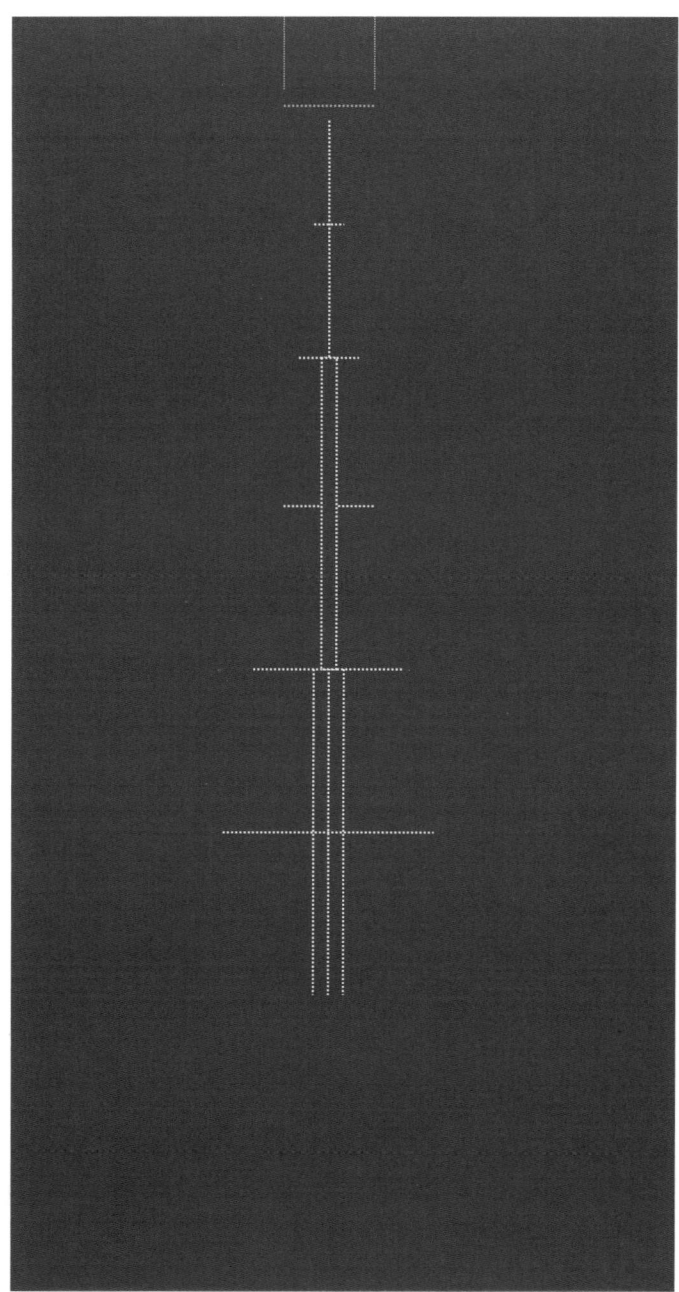

Fig 8.9 Approach lighting runway category I

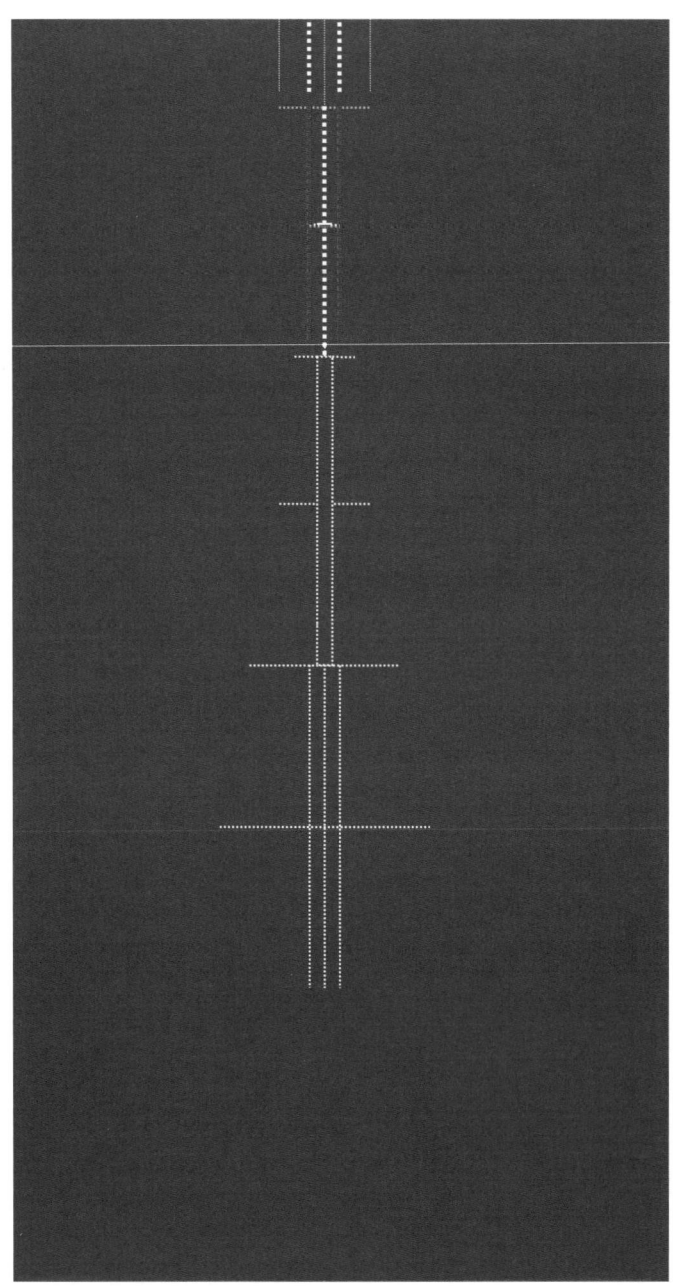

Fig 8.10 Precision approach lighting runway category II & III

Precision Approach Runway Category II and III

This is more complicated, with red barrettes close to the runway, and is shown in figure 8.10.

Precision Approach Path Indicator (PAPI)

The PAPI system, and the derived APAPI system, gives pilots on instrument approaches precision indication of their approach path in elevation. It consists of a **wing bar** of 4 lights or light pairs at the side of the runway, each of which appears to change colour quite suddenly from red to white as the approach angle increases. The angles of the light transition are arranged so that small changes in approach angle are indicated by changes in the number of lights of each colour seen by the pilot. If he is on the correct path, he should see 2 red lights close to the runway and 2 white lights outside them. If his approach angle is a little too steep and he is high on the approach, he will see **3 white lights** outside one red light. If well above the approach path he will see 4 white lights. If he is **slightly below** the slope, he will see 3 red lights inside one white light, and if well below the approach path, and **dangerously low**, he will see **4 red lights**. There may be a bar on each side of the runway.

8.10 Signs

Signs (vertical boards with writing on them) provide pilots with information. They are either mandatory signs or information signs. **Mandatory** signs are the only ones using red as a background, on which the writing is in white.

Mandatory Signs

These are provided to give an instruction which pilots must obey unless instructed by air traffic services. They include **STOP** signs, **NO ENTRY** signs, holding position signs, category I, II or III holding position signs, and other taxiway/runway intersection signs. They are illuminated at night.

Taxi-holding Position Signs

These are used when taxi-holding positions are marked on the surface. Figure 8.11(a) below (which also shows a non-mandatory location sign) indicates a normal taxi-holding position. Figure 8.11 (b) indicates the runway and the approach category for which the taxi-holding position applies. Signs at taxi-holding positions away from runway or taxiway intersections are marked with a designator as in figure 8.11(c).

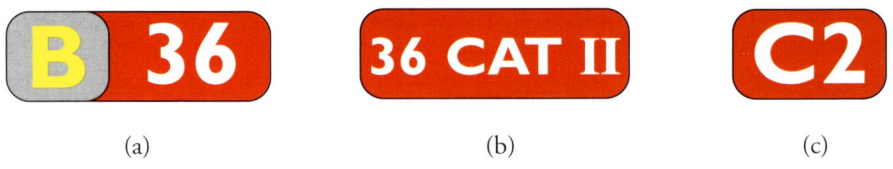

(a) (b) (c)

FIGURE 8.11 TAXI-HOLDING POSITION SIGNS

Road-holding Position Sign

As a mandatory sign, it will be in **white on a red background**, explaining the need to stop and obtain clearance from ATC if necessary.

Information Signs

These identify a specific location or routing information. A **location** sign is yellow on a black background, as the sign forming part of the taxi-holding position sign at figure 8.11(a). Other information signs are in black on a yellow background. They might be destination signs (showing the route to a runway or important feature), direction signs (indicating a taxiway route designator), runway exits, or runway vacated signs. Examples are shown in figure 8.12.

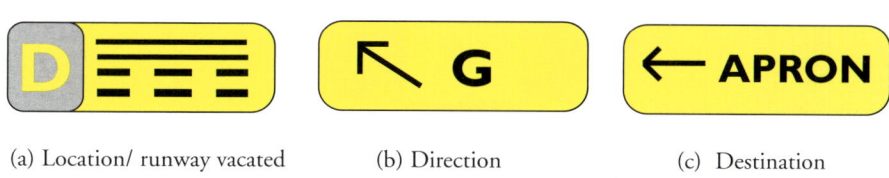

(a) Location/ runway vacated   (b) Direction   (c) Destination

Fig 8.12 Information signs

8.11 Markers

Markers are objects placed in position to indicate information. They should be lightweight and frangible, and low enough to cause no problem to propellers or jet pods. They are usually used to mark unpaved surfaces.

Runway Markers

Conical markers or flat rectangular ones laid parallel to the runway direction, may mark the **edge of an unlit runway**.

Taxiway Markers

If there are no taxiway lights as part of the markers, they will be **retroflective** (reflective), where taxiway lights ought to be, in the form of cones.

Boundary Markers

If there is no runway at an aerodrome, conical or wedge shaped boundary markers (often red and white), may be provided.

8.12 Marking Obstacles

Obstacles on or near an airfield which cannot be eliminated must be **marked, and lit at night**. They should be painted **red**, or orange, with **white** as a colour contrast, in a chequer pattern, or in bands. If the obstacle cannot be coloured, it should have a marker or flag put on or next to it. There will be markers on **overhead wires**, at least as high as the highest point of the wire.

Fig 8.13 Chequer pattern

Obstacle Lights

There are 3 different types of obstacle lights: low intensity, medium intensity, and high intensity. Low intensity lights (normally steady red) are used for obstacles less than 45 metres high. Medium intensity lights (flashing red or white) are used for higher, or extensive, obstacles. On obstacles more than 150 metres high, and on some towers supporting wires, high intensity lights (flashing white) are used by day as well as night. Lights are placed at the tops of obstacles, and usually at 45 metre spacing down from the top. High intensity lights on obstacles which do not support cables all flash together, whereas lights on high obstacles which do support overhead wires flash in sequence middle, top, bottom. Mobile obstructions have flashing yellow or red lights, although security vehicles use blue.

8.13 Restricted Use Area Markings

Closed parts of Runways and Taxiways

Large crosses on the surface mark each end of closed parts of runways and taxiways, and may also be placed at intervals along a closed runway. They will be white on runways and yellow on taxiways. If a taxiway touches the closed area, red lights indicate the closed parts at night.

Non-load-bearing Surfaces

Where the edge of a taxiway, holding bay or apron cannot safely bear the load of an aircraft, it is marked with double unbroken yellow lines.

Pre-threshold Area

A paved area before the start of the runway which is unsuitable for normal movement of aircraft is marked as such by yellow (or other non-white contrasting colour) chevrons leading to the threshold, as figure 8.14.

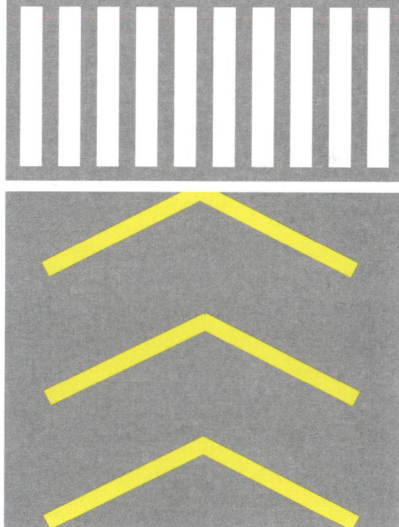

FIG 8.14 UNSUITABLE PAVED AREA

8.14 Emergency Services

Every aerodrome has a **rescue and fire fighting service**, whose principle objective is to **save lives**. The most important factors in effective rescue after a survivable aircraft accident are: the training received by the personnel, the effectiveness of the equipment, and the speed with which the personnel and equipment can be put into use.

Aerodrome Category for Rescue and Firefighting

The necessary level of protection is based on the assessed danger from an aircraft accident. Each aerodrome is categorised by a number depending on the length of the aircraft which normally use it (the fuselage width is also considered). That category is used to determine the level of firefighting and rescue protection provided.

Response Time

The response time is the time between the initial call to the rescue and fire-fighting service, and the time when a fire vehicle is in position to pump a certain rate of foam at the danger. The response time should be 2 minutes, and in any case not more than 3 minutes, to the end of any runway or any part of the movement area (in good conditions).

8.15 Apron Management Services

Priority of Movement on an Apron

Emergency vehicles responding to an emergency have priority over all other traffic on the apron. Aircraft (including those being pushed or towed) have priority over vehicles at other times, of course.

8.16 Safety During Ground Servicing

There is always a danger of fuel spillage and possible fire when aircraft are being serviced. Fire extinguishing equipment and personnel trained in its use must be readily available during such ground servicing. There must be a way to summon the rescue and fire-fighting service quickly in the event of a fire or a major fuel spill.

8.17 Definitions

You are required to distinguish most of the definitions of words listed in Annex 14. Many of them you will know already, and some have been wholly or partially defined in the text already. Here is a list of the full definitions of the words you are required to distinguish.

The Aerodrome and its Parts

AERODROME
*A defined area on land or water (including any buildings, installations and equipment) intended to be **used either wholly or in part for the arrival, departure, and surface movement of aircraft.***

HELIPORT
An aerodrome or a defined area on a structure intended to be used wholly or in part for the arrival, departure and surface movement of helicopters.

AERODROME REFERENCE POINT
The designated geographical location of an aerodrome.

AERODROME ELEVATION
The elevation of the highest point of the landing area.

LANDING AREA
That part of a movement area intended for the landing and taking off of aircraft.

MOVEMENT AREA
That part of the aerodrome to be used for the take-off, landing and taxiing of aircraft, consisting of the manoeuvring area and the apron(s).

MANOEUVRING AREA
That part of the aerodrome to be used for the take-off, landing and taxiing of aircraft, excluding aprons.

APRON
A defined area, on a land aerodrome, intended to accommodate aircraft for the purposes of loading or unloading passengers, mail or cargo, fuelling, parking or maintenance.

Aircraft stand
A designated area on an apron intended to be used for the parking of aircraft.

Taxiway
A defined path on a land aerodrome established for the taxiing of aircraft and intended to provide a link between one part of the aerodrome and another.

Taxiway intersection
A junction of two or more taxiways.

Taxiway strip
An area including a taxiway intended to protect an aircraft operating on the taxiway and to reduce the risk of damage to an aircraft accidentally running off the taxiway.

Holding bay
A defined area where aircraft can be held, or bypassed, to facilitate efficient surface movement of aircraft.

Taxi-holding position
A designated position at which taxiing aircraft and other vehicles shall stop and hold position, unless otherwise authorised by the aerodrome control tower.

Road
An established surface route on the movement area meant for the exclusive use of vehicles.

Road-holding position
A designated position at which vehicles may be required to hold.

Runway guard lights
A light system intended to caution pilots or vehicle drivers that they are about to enter an active runway.

Runway
A defined rectangular area on a land aerodrome prepared for the landing and taking off of aircraft.

Runway strip
A defined area including the runway and stopway, if provided, intended:

    a. to reduce the risk of damage to aircraft running off a runway; and
    b. to protect aircraft flying over it during take-off or landing operations.

Shoulder
An area adjacent to the edge of a pavement so prepared as to provide a transition between the pavement and the adjacent land surface.

Runway end safety area (RESA)
An area symmetrical about the extended runway centre line and adjacent to the end of the strip primarily intended to reduce the risk of damage to an aeroplane undershooting or overrunning the runway.

Stopway
A defined rectangular area on the ground at the end of the take-off run available prepared as a suitable area in which an aircraft can be stopped in the case of an abandoned take-off.

Clearway
A defined rectangular area on the ground or water under the control of the appropriate authority, selected or prepared as a suitable area over which an aeroplane may make a portion of its initial climb to a specified height.

Runway Descriptions

Primary runway(s)
Runway(s) used in preference to others whenever conditions permit.

Take-off runway
A runway intended for take-off only.

Instrument runway
A runway intended for the operation of aircraft using instrument approach procedures.

Non-instrument runway
A runway intended for the operation of aircraft using visual approach procedures.

Parts of a Runway

THRESHOLD   *The beginning of that portion of the runway usable for landing.*

DISPLACED THRESHOLD   *A threshold not located at an extremity of a runway.*

TOUCHDOWN ZONE
The portion of a runway, beyond the threshold, where it is intended that landing aeroplanes first contact the runway.

Declared Distances

TAKE-OFF RUN AVAILABLE (TORA)
The length of runway declared available and suitable for the ground run of an aeroplane taking off.

TAKE-OFF DISTANCE AVAILABLE (TODA)
The length of the take-off run available plus the length of the clearway, if provided.

ACCELERATE STOP DISTANCE AVAILABLE (ASDA)
The length of the take-off run available plus the length of the stopway, if provided.

LANDING DISTANCE AVAILABLE (LDA)
The length of runway which is declared available and suitable for the ground run of an aeroplane landing.

Undesirables

Slush
Water-saturated snow which with a heel-and -toe slap-down motion against the ground will be displaced with a splatter; specific gravity: 0.5 up to 0.8.

Dry snow
Snow which can be blown if loose or, if compacted by hand, will fall apart again upon release; specific gravity: up to but not including 0.35.

Wet snow
Snow which, if compacted by hand, will stick together and tend to or form a snowball; specific gravity: 0.35 up to but not including 0.5.

Compacted snow
Snow which has been compressed into a solid mass that resists further compression and will hold together or break up into lumps if picked up; specific gravity: 0.5 and over.

Obstacle
All fixed (whether temporary or permanent) and mobile objects, or parts thereof, that are located on an area intended for the surface movement of aircraft or that extend above a defined surface intended to protect aircraft in flight.

Frangible object
An object of low mass designed to break, distort, or yield on impact so as to present the minimum hazard to aircraft.

Lights and Markers

Aeronautical ground light
Any light specially provided as an aid to air navigation, other than a light displayed on an aircraft.

Aeronautical beacon
An aeronautical ground light visible in all azimuths, either continuously or intermittently, to designate a particular point on the surface of the earth.

AERODROME BEACON
An aeronautical beacon used to indicate the location of an aerodrome from the air.

IDENTIFICATION BEACON
An aeronautical beacon emitting a coded signal by means of which a particular point of reference can be identified.

AERODROME IDENTIFICATION SIGN
A sign placed on an aerodrome to aid in identifying the aerodrome from the air.

LANDING DIRECTION INDICATOR
A device to indicate visually the direction currently designated for landing and for take-off.

HAZARD BEACON
An aeronautical beacon used to designate a danger to air navigation

FIXED LIGHT
A light having constant luminous intensity when viewed from a fixed point.

CAPACITOR DISCHARGE LIGHT
A lamp in which high-intensity flashes of extremely short duration are produced by the discharge of electricity at high voltage through a gas enclosed in a tube.

BARRETTE
Three or more aeronautical ground lights closely spaced in a traverse line so that from a distance they appear as a short bar of light.

SIGNAL AREA
An area on an aerodrome used for the display of ground signals.

MARKER
An object displayed above ground level in order to indicate an obstacle or delineate a boundary.

MARKING
A symbol or group of symbols displayed on the surface of the movement area in order to convey aeronautical information.

8.18 Exercise

1. The 'aerodrome reference code' is referred to in Annex 14 and other ICAO documents. What is the purpose of the code?

    a. To describe the rescue and firefighting facilities at the aerodrome
    b. To describe the expected weather factor at the aerodrome
    c. To describe the type of aircraft the aerodrome is intended to serve
    d. To describe the length of the primary runway at the aerodrome

2. Which of the following is not one of the main declared runway distances at an aerodrome?

    a. Take-off run available
    b. Landing run available
    c. Take-off distance available
    d. Landing distance available

3. Which of the following is defined as "The length of the take-off run available plus the length of the stopway, if provided"?

    a. Takeoff distance available
    b. Landing distance available
    c. Landing run available
    d. Accelerate stop distance available

4. Which are the defined states of frozen water on a runway which may affect aircraft performance?

    a. Ice, snow, frost
    b. Ice, slush, snow
    c. Slush, snow, frost
    d. Ice, frost, slush

5. How should the state of the runway surface be reported if the runway surface is soaked, but there is no standing water?

    a. Runway surface dry
    b. Runway surface wet
    c. Runway surface damp
    d. Runway surface soaked

6. Which of the following correctly describes a runway surface which is reported as having 'water patches'?

   a. Extensive patches of standing water are visible
   b. Occasional patches of standing water are visible
   c. Significant patches of standing water are visible
   d. Water floods the runway but flows off quickly

7. What shape and colour is a landing direction indicator?

   a. A white capital T ; land along the stem towards the crosspiece
   b. An orange or red windsock, land towards the mast
   c. A white or orange capital T, land along the stem towards the crosspiece
   d. An orange wedge shape in 3 dimensions, land towards the point of the wedge

8. Which of the following capabilities is not required by ICAO recommended practice from a signal lamp?

   a. It must be capable of signalling in 3 colours simultaneously
   b. It must be able to flash morse messages in any of 3 colours
   c. It must have a narrow beamwidth of less than 3 degrees
   d. The 3 colours specified are green, red and white

9. How would you recognise an aiming point marking on a runway?

   a. 2 thick yellow lines close to and parallel to the runway centreline
   b. 2 thick white lines close to and parallel to the runway centreline
   c. 2 pairs of yellow lines close to and parallel to the runway centreline
   d. 2 pairs of white lines close to and parallel to the runway centreline

10. On a normal aerodrome, what colour should apron safety lines be painted?

    a. White
    b. Yellow
    c. Any colour which contrasts with the surface
    d. Any colour which contrasts with the aircraft stand markings

11. What is the meaning of the marking below when seen on a taxiway?

    a. Taxiway intersection ahead. Give way to crossing aircraft
    b. Taxiway intersection ahead. Stop unless cleared by air traffic control
    c. Taxi-holding position. Stop unless cleared by air traffic control
    d. Taxi-holding position category II & III. Stop during these operations

12. What colour are (i) taxiway edge lights and (ii) runway edge lights?

    a. (i) yellow   (ii) white
    b. (i) green   (ii) white
    c. (i) blue   (ii) white
    d. (i) green   (ii) yellow

13. What lights will a pilot see from the PAPI system if he is slightly low on the instrument approach glideslope? Inboard means closer to the runway.

    a. 3 white lights inboard of 1 red light
    b. 3 red lights inboard of 1 white light
    c. 1 white light inboard of 3 red lights
    d. 1 red light inboard of 3 white lights

14. How can a pilot determine from a distance that an aerodrome sign contains mandatory instructions?

    a. The writing will be red on a white background
    b. The writing will be white on a red background
    c. The sign will be outlined in yellow and black stripes
    d. The sign will be yellow on a black background, or vice versa.

15. How should a closed part of a runway be marked?

    a. With yellow and black marker boards
    b. With red and white marker boards
    c. With a white cross on the surface
    d. With white chevrons on the surface

16. What is the response time for which an aerodrome rescue and firefighting service should aim?

   a. 1 minute, but with a maximum of 2 minutes
   b. 2 minutes, but with a maximum of 3 minutes
   c. 3 minutes at all times
   d. 3 minutes, but with a maximum of 5 minutes

17. What is the principle objective of a rescue and firefighting service?

   a. To prevent the spread of fire to other aircraft and facilities
   b. To minimise the damage caused by fire
   c. To extinguish any fire with the minimum delay
   d. To save lives

Chapter 9

Accident Investigation

9.1 Introduction

The news media regularly alert us to the unpleasant fact that aircraft accidents continue to occur. For international operations ICAO clarifies, in Annex 13, who is to investigate what, and how. These procedures are recommended for all operations, and apply everywhere.

In the UK, the pilot (or operator if the pilot cannot) is required to report all accidents to the police and to the Aircraft Accident Investigation Branch of the Department for Transport, and serious incidents to the Safety Investigation and Data Department of the Safety Regulation Group of the CAA (Civil Aviation Authority). They are encouraged to report all incidents, so that safety lessons may be learned from them. Incidents may also be reported under the independent Confidential Human Factors Incident Reporting Programme (CHIRP).

9.2 Investigations

The responsibility for investigating an accident or incident lies with the State (the State of Occurrence) in or over whose territory (or agreed area of responsibility if over the high seas) the accident occurs. Hence, Scotland instituted the investigation into the Lockerbie bombing. If there is doubt as to where it happened, the State of Registry takes on the responsibility, as it does if the accident occurs in a State which is not contracted to ICAO. However, the State of Occurrence may delegate responsibility for carrying out all or part of that investigation to the State of Registry.

The basic aim of the investigation is not to apportion blame, but to prevent future accidents or incidents.

9.3 Accidents

An accident is defined in Annex 13 as *an occurrence associated with the operation of an aircraft which takes place between the time any person boards the aircraft with the intention of flight until such time as all such persons have disembarked, in which*

a) *a person is fatally or seriously injured as a result of being in the aircraft, OR direct contact with any part of the aircraft, including parts which have become detached from the aircraft, OR direct exposure to jet blast.*

(except when the injuries are from natural causes, self-inflicted or inflicted by other persons, or when the injuries are to stowaways hiding outside the areas normally available to the passengers and crew); OR

b) *the aircraft sustains damage or structural failure which:*
adversely affects the structural strength, performance or flight characteristics of the aircraft, AND
would normally require major repair or replacement of the affected component.

(except for engine failure or damage, when the damage is limited to the engine, its cowlings or accessories; or for damage limited to propellers, wingtips, antennae, tyres, brakes, fairings, small dents or puncture holes in the aircraft skin), OR

c) *the aircraft is missing or is completely inaccessible.*

This definition may appear daunting, but you do not have to remember it exactly; you need only understand and reproduce the gist of it.

Think of it in basic terms; it is an accident if something happens to **cause death or serious injury**, or damage to an aircraft which affects its **structural strength** or **flight characteristics**.

Consider such injury or damage as **destroying** a person or an aircraft, or putting either of them **into hospital (or the hangar) for major repair**.

Of course if either a person or the aircraft is **inaccessible**, one must assume the worst.

The accident must happen either **on** or as **a result of touching** the **aircraft** or a **part** of it (including parts which have fallen off), or efflux produced by it, or **by reason of being** in the aircraft.

It must also happen while the aircraft is in flight, preparing for flight, or recovering from flight, in that the timing is between the first person who intends flying getting into the aircraft, and the last person getting out after a flight (completed or intended).

Death from natural causes, or self-inflicted injury are accepted as not being accidental. Of course deliberate damage is not accidental, but an aircraft shot down can still be considered as accidentally damaged!

Minor injuries, or easily repaired damage (especially to a replaceable engine) are not considered serious enough to warrant the description of an accident, but can be attributed to an incident, perhaps a serious incident.

9.4 Serious Incidents

The definition of a serious incident is deceptively simple - *an incident involving circumstances indicating that an accident nearly occurred.* The only difference between an accident and a serious incident is the **result**. Therefore it is treated almost as seriously, and must be investigated as carefully. Of course, the devil is not in the detail so much as in the simplicity; who decides if an accident "nearly occurred"? Fortunately, Annex 13 lists as an attachment some examples of serious incidents. You may have to consider an occurrence, and decide whether it is an accident or a serious incident.

Some examples of serious incidents follow, but are far from exhaustive:

- Near collisions requiring a manoeuvre to avoid an unsafe situation. *(In the UK these are called "Airproxes", and are reported to and investigated by the independent UK Airprox Board)*
- Controlled flight into terrain only marginally avoided.
- Attempted use of a closed or 'occupied' runway.
- Gross failures to achieve calculated performance during take-off or initial climb.
- Fire or smoke in the cabin, cargo compartment or engine.
- Flight crew incapacitation in flight (but not as bad as serious injury).
- Aircraft structural failures not classified as accidents
  (not affecting structural strength).
- Engine disintegrations not classified as accidents (no structural damage).

- Multiple malfunctions of aircraft systems seriously affecting aircraft operation (but not requiring repair or replacement of flight controls - that would be an accident).
- Take-off or landing incidents, such as undershooting, overrunning, or running off the runway side.
- System failures, weather phenomena, flight outside the approved flight envelope or other occurrences which could have caused difficulties controlling the aircraft.
- Low fuel state such that the pilot has to declare an emergency.

9.5 Serious Injury

Serious injuries are defined at length in para 6, and unfortunately you may have to recognise that definition and perhaps discriminate between serious injury and minor injury. To assist with the definition, here again is a fairly simple guide.

Basically, an injury is serious if it happens in an accident and entails **hospitalisation for more than 48 hours**. (The injured person must decide to go to hospital within 7 days of the accident.)

Modern surgical techniques allow swift discharge from hospital. If that happens, it is still considered a serious injury if a bone is fractured, or an **internal organ** is injured, or a person is **badly burned**, exposed to **radiation** or **infection**, or 'lacerations' (skin damage) cause **severe bleeding, nerve, muscle or tendon** damage.

Exceptions are simple fractures (no skin broken or internal damage) to the nose, finger or toe, and first degree burns to less than 5% of the body surface.

9.6 Definitions

You will know many of the following definitions, and some are explained in the text. However, you are expected to distinguish them all.

AIRCRAFT
Any machine that can derive support in the atmosphere from the reactions of the air other than the reactions of the air against the earth's surface.

OPERATOR
A person, organisation or enterprise engaged in or offering to engage in aircraft operations.

STATE OF REGISTRY
The State on whose register the aircraft is entered.

STATE OF THE OPERATOR
The state in which the operator's principal place of business is located, or if there is no such place of business, the operator's permanent residence,

STATE OF OCCURRENCE
The State in the territory of which an accident or incident occurs.

ACCIDENT
The definition of an accident is given in the text. You will be expected to know the definition only in general terms.

INCIDENT
An occurrence, other than an accident, associated with the operation of an aircraft which affects or could affect the safety of operation.

SERIOUS INCIDENT
An incident involving circumstances indicating that an accident nearly occurred.

AIRPROX
(UK definition) A situation where a person considers the safety of an aircraft has been compromised by the proximity of another aircraft.

Serious Injury
A description of what constitutes serious injury is given in the text, but the definition is written here in full. *An injury sustained by a person in an accident and which;*

> *requires hospitalisation for more than 48 hours commencing within 7 days from the date when the injury is received, or*
> *results in a fracture of any bone (except simple fractures of fingers, toes or nose) or involves lacerations which cause severe haemorrhage, nerve, muscle or tendon damage, or*
> *involves injury to any internal organs or*
> *involves second or third degree burns, or any burns affecting more than 5 per cent of the body surface or*
> *involves verified exposure to infectious substances or injurious radiation.*

Investigation
A process conducted for the purpose of accident prevention which includes the gathering and analysis of information, the drawing of conclusions, including the determination of causes, and, when appropriate, the making of safety recommendations.

Flight Recorder
Any type of recorder installed in the aircraft for the purpose of complementing accident/incident investigation.

9.7　Exercise

1. What is the objective of an accident investigation?

   a. To determine the cause
   b. To apportion blame
   c. To determine whether any law was broken
   d. To prevent future accidents

2. Which of the following occurrences to an aircraft in flight should be considered an aviation accident? Assume no further damage or injury is caused beyond that described.

   a. An engine disintegrates but causes no further damage
   b. A wingtip is broken off in a collision
   c. One passenger is stabbed by another
   d. A passenger suffers second degree burns from a loose galley kettle

3. Which of the following occurrences to an aircraft in flight should be considered a serious incident? Assume no further damage or injury is caused beyond that described.

   a. An engine disintegrates and prevents flap retraction
   b. A passenger is taken ill with an infectious disease
   c. The pilot takes avoiding action to prevent a near collision
   d. A crew member falls in turbulence and breaks his leg.

4. Which of the following occurrences to an aircraft in flight should be considered an aviation accident? Assume no further damage or injury is caused beyond that described.

   a. An extinguished engine fire damages the engine oil system.
   b. One pilot is incapacitated by food poisoning for 36 hours
   c. An undercarriage leg requires replacement after a heavy landing
   d. An aborted take-off bursts 6 tyres.

5. Which of the following correctly defines an "aircraft"?

   a. A power-driven heavier than air machine, deriving its lift in flight chiefly from aerodynamic reactions on surfaces which remain fixed under given conditions of flight
   b. Any machine that can derive support in the atmosphere from the reactions of the air other than the reactions of the air against the earth's surface
   c. A power driven machine which derives support in the atmosphere from the pressure of the air against its structure.
   d. A power driven machine deriving its lift in flight chiefly from the reactions of the air other than the reactions of the air against the earth's surface

6. Where do the specifications in Annex 13 not apply?

   a. Over the high seas
   b. Over the territory of the State of registry
   c. In the territory of a non-contracting state
   d. They apply in all of the above

Chapter 10

Search & Rescue

10.1 Introduction

Passengers tend to have a fear of surviving a crash landing and not being rescued. Tales of cannibalism in the Andes have only made things worse. It is therefore important that wherever aircraft fly, there is an organisation set up to find survivors and rescue them as quickly as possible. ICAO Annex 12 lays down the standards and recommended practices for search and rescue services.

10.2 Responsibility

Over land or the territorial waters of an individual State, that State is responsible for providing the necessary service. (Regional agreements establish who looks after specific parts of the high seas.) The responsible State must provide a 24 hour search and rescue service for every aircraft, whatever the nationality of the aircraft or survivors.

Search and Rescue (SAR) Regions in which States agree to provide such services are usually the same as the Flight Information Regions, whose ATS units will provide the alerting service (see Chapter 7). Inside each Region, there is a Rescue Coordination Centre (RCC).

10.3 Rescue Units

Rescue units, with trained personnel and suitable equipment, are located to cover the whole search and rescue region. They have facilities for locating crashed aircraft and survivors and for providing assistance for them. They are able to communicate with the RCC and should be able to communicate with each other; although that does not have to mean by radio, it may be by telephone or similar.

Search and rescue aircraft are able to communicate by radio on 121.5 MHz and 243 MHz. They carry homing devices for locator beacons, and at least one aircraft in each SAR region can carry droppable survival equipment.

10.4   Co-operation

SAR procedures, plans and operations are co-ordinated with neighbouring States, in accordance with ICAO standards and recommended practices.

All aircraft and vessels are instructed to co-operate fully with the SAR organisation and to provide assistance to survivors. States are recommended to inform their populations how to report a possible aircraft accident.

10.5   SAR Emergency Phases

There are 3 **"emergency phases"** of SAR operations. The first is the **"uncertainty phase"**, abbreviated to INCERFA. This means the RCC is told that there MAY be a problem with an aircraft requiring SAR operations. (For example, communication lost for 30 minutes). The next is the **"alert phase"** or "ALERFA", when for example an aircraft is still not in radio contact, or has not landed within 5 minutes of receiving clearance, or has been hijacked. Finally, the **"distress phase"** or DETRESFA applies when the aircraft is known to have made or be about to make a crash landing or ditching. These phases are decided not by the RCC but by the responsible ATS unit.

10.6   Action by Pilots in Command at an Accident Scene

If a pilot sees another aircraft (or a surface craft) in distress, he must try to keep it in sight until he is no longer needed. He is to report to the local RCC or ATS unit, including, if possible, the type and identification of the craft in distress, the **position** and **time** of sighting, the **number of persons** visible, and whether they have **abandoned** their craft, in which case **how many are floating** in water, and their apparent **condition**. The pilot should then follow the RCC or ATS unit's instructions.

The PiC of the **first** aircraft on the scene is to **take charge** until the arrival of a SAR aircraft, unless he has to hand over to another aircraft for communications reasons. If he needs to direct a surface craft to the scene without the use of radio, he is to use the signals at para 10.8. To pass information to survivors, he should drop a radio if he has one, or a written message. He is to acknowledge signals to the aircraft as in para 10.9.

10.7 Pilot in Command Intercepting a Distress Message

If a pilot intercepts a distress message, he is to try to obtain a **bearing** on the transmission, and note any position given. If the message is not acknowledged by an ATS unit or a RCC, he is to relay to the RCC or ATS unit all he has received, and **await instructions**, while going **to the reported position** at his own discretion.

10.8 Signalling to Surface Craft

To direct a surface vessel in a given direction without radio communication, an aircraft must first **circle** the vessel at least once, then **fly low across** the vessel's **bows** (at a safe distance) while **rocking its wings** and making **noises** by varying throttle setting or changing the pitch of its propeller. Having attracted attention, the pilot should fly **in the direction** he wants the vessel to follow.

If the pilot **no longer needs** the vessel's assistance, he should **cross astern** of the vessel at low level, again rocking his wings and varying engine or propeller noise.

The vessel may respond **by flashing a succession of 'T's in morse (all dashes), or** hoisting a **red and white vertically striped** pennant, **or just by turning to follow**. **If it** cannot comply **for some reason, it will signal a succession of morse 'N's (alternate dash and dot)** or hoisting a **blue and white chequered** pennant.

10.9 Ground to Air Visual Code

Survivors may use any means at their disposal to make marks in the shape of the following symbols to be visible to aircraft. Pilots must be aware of their meaning, and remember they may appear different from different directions.

V	I require assistance
X	I require medical assistance
N	No or Negative
Y	Yes or Affirmative
↑	I am proceeding in this direction

A pilot seeing any of these symbols should proceed as in para 10.7 above, and acknowledge that he **understands** the symbol by **rocking his wings**, or at night **flashing** his landing lights (or navigation lights) **twice**. Note this is the same acknowledgement signal as given to an interceptor.

Other ground to air signals made by rescue teams are in the table below.

LLL	Operation Completed
LL	We have found all personnel
++	We have found only some personnel
XX	We are not able to continue, returning to base
←→ (arrows diverging)	Have divided into 2 groups, each going in direction indicated
→→	Information received that aircraft is in this direction
NN	Nothing found, will continue to search

10.10 **Definitions**

You will be required to distinguish the following definitions, some of which you already know and most of which have been explained.

OPERATOR
A person, organisation or enterprise engaged in or offering to engage in aircraft operation.

PILOT-IN-COMMAND
The pilot responsible for the operation and safety of the aircraft during flight time.

STATE OF REGISTRY
The State on whose register the aircraft is entered.

RESCUE UNIT
A unit composed of trained personnel and provided with equipment suitable for the expeditious conduct of search and rescue.

RESCUE CO-ORDINATION CENTRE
A unit responsible for promoting efficient organisation of search and rescue service and for co-ordinating the conduct of search and rescue operations within a search and rescue region.

RADIO DIRECTION-FINDING STATION
A radio station intended to determine only the direction of other stations by means of transmissions from the latter.

EMERGENCY PHASE
A generic term meaning, as the case may be, uncertainty phase, alert phase, or distress phase.

UNCERTAINTY PHASE
A situation wherein uncertainty exists as to the safety of an aircraft and its occupants.

ALERT PHASE
A situation wherein apprehension exists as to the safety of an aircraft and its occupants.

DISTRESS PHASE
A situation wherein there is a reasonable certainty that an aircraft and its occupants are threatened by grave and imminent danger or require immediate assistance.

INTENTIONALLY LEFT BLANK

10.11 Exercise

1. Who is responsible for providing search and rescue facilities over land?

   a. The State of Registry of the aircraft
   b. The State from which the aircraft took off
   c. The State in whose territory the crash occurred
   d. ICAO

2. Who is responsible for providing SAR facilities over the high seas?

   a. ICAO
   b. The State which accepts responsibility under a regional agreement
   c. The State of Registry of the aircraft involved
   d. The State over whose territory the aircraft last flew

3. According to ICAO Annex 12, what should States require aircraft and vessels registered in their State to do without being specifically requested?

   a. To inform RCCs of their position at regular intervals
   b. To listen on VHF emergency frequency 121.5 MHz at all times
   c. To provide all facilities for survivors
   d. To transport accident investigators to the scene of an accident

4. If the pilot of an aircraft in contact with an ATS unit observes a vessel or aircraft in distress, he must report it to the ATS unit. Which of the following facts does he not need to attempt to ascertain and include in his report?

   a. The identification of the vessel in distress
   b. The number of persons in the water, if any
   c. The time of sighting in UTC
   d. The positions of any other vessels in sight

5. How should a pilot attract the attention of a surface vessel to indicate that he wishes it to go in a particular direction?

   a. By flying alongside the vessel and rocking his wings
   b. By circling and flying low across the path of the vessel (in front of it)
   c. By circling and flying low across the wake of the vessel (behind it)
   d. By flying alongside the vessel and turning sharply away

6. If a pilot sees the following 2.5 metre symbol on the ground, what does it mean? **X**

   a. A survivor requires medical assistance
   b. A survivor requires general assistance
   c. This is a safe spot for dropping SAR equipment
   d. Negative

7. If a pilot sees the symbol at question 6 above, how can he tell the survivor that he understands the message?

   a. Fly low past the symbol and turn away sharply
   b. Rock his wings
   c. Fly in circles around the symbol
   d. Fly low past the symbol and climb steeply

8. Which symbol indicates that the survivors have left the scene of a crash?

   a. Y
   b. V
   c. ↓
   d. N

9. What is correctly defined as "A situation wherein apprehension exists as to the safety of an aircraft and its occupants"?

   a. The emergency phase
   b. The uncertainty phase
   c. The alert phase
   d. The distress phase

10. If a pilot sees the following 2.5 metre symbol on the ground, what does it mean? **Z**

    a. A survivor requires medical assistance
    b. The survivors have been rescued
    c. Affirmative
    d. Negative

Answers to Exercises

Chapters 1 - 10

Chapter 1	Chapter 2	Chapter 3	Chapter 4	Chapter 5
1. c 2. d 3. c 4. c 5. c 6. c 7. a 8. d	1. c 2. c 3. d 4. d	1. d 2. c 3. b 4. d 5. d 6. c 7. d 8. d 9. b	1. b 2. d 3. d 4. d 5. c 6. b	1. b 2. c 3. b 4. a 5. d 6. b 7. a 8. d 9. b 10. b 11. d 12. c 13. b 14. c* *(see para 3.11)
Chapter 6	Chapter 7	Chapter 8	Chapter 9	Chapter 10
1. d 2. d 3. d 4. a 5. a 6. a 7. d 8. c 9. d 10. a 11. b	1. c 2. a 3. b 4. d 5. b 6. a 7. c 8. b 9. d 10. b 11. b 12. d 13. d	1. c 2. b 3. d 4. b 5. b 6. c 7. c 8. a 9. b 10. d 11. d 12. c 13. b 14. b 15. c 16. b 17. d	1. d 2. d 3. c 4. c 5. b 6. d	1. c 2. b 3. c 4. d 5. b 6. a 7. b 8. c 9. c 10. d

INTENTIONALLY LEFT BLANK

Index

A

ACAS	75, 80
accelerate stop distance available	89, 114
accident	73, 110, 122
accident actions	121, 130
accident investigation	121, 126
accident report	121
advisory airspace	35, 37, 71, 77
aerodrome	1, 49, 62, 71, 72, 87, 110
aerodrome beacon	98, 116
aerodrome category	110
Aerodrome Traffic Zone	72, 77
Aeronautical Information Publication	1, 69, 78
aeroplane	24, 62
AIC	16
AIP	1, 69, 72, 78
Air Navigation Order	4
air traffic	63
Air Traffic Control	76
Air Traffic Services	73, 78
aircraft	62
aircraft stand	87, 97, 112
Airep Special	73
Airfield and Runway Lighting	98
Airprox	123, 125
airship	24
airspace classification	71
airway	71, 76
airworthiness	9, 15
ALERFA	130
alert	130, 133
Alerting Service	73, 77
alternate aerodrome	37, 81
altimeter setting	36, 73
altitude	35, 36, 39, 64
anti-collision beacons	26
approach lights	102
apron	62, 91, 95, 110
ASDA	89, 114
assembly	34, 39
ATZ	72

B

balloon	24, 26
barometric pressure	36

C

ceiling	65
Certificate of Airworthiness	3, 9
Certificate of Maintenance Review	10, 15
Certificate of Registration	3
Certificate of Release to Service	10
Chicago Convention	1, 69
classification of airspace	71
clearance	79
clearway	89, 93, 113
cloud	32, 35, 65
collision risk	23, 27
commander	15, 17, 31, 40, 52, 63, 130
congested area	16, 34, 39
control area	71, 76
control zone	71, 76
controlled airspace	1, 35, 37, 40, 71, 76
converging	24
cruising altitudes	35
cruising level	37, 64
currency	19, 20
customs duty	3

D

Danger Area	70, 77
declared distances	88, 114
definitions	62, 111, 125, 133
DETRESFA	130
differences	1, 4, 31
differences training	17
displaced threshold	88, 96, 114
distress	46, 51, 75, 130, 131, 133
divert	49, 81
documents to be carried	12

E

EASA	4, 9
emergency	73, 75, 88, 110
emergency phase	133
emergency phases	130
endangering	70
equipment to be carried	11, 37
estimated time of arrival	80
European Aviation Safety Agency	4, 9

F

facilitation	3
fire fighting	110
Flight Information Region	77, 129
Flight Information Service	72, 73, 77
flight level	36, 64
flight plan	35, 37, 73, 79
flight time	20
flying machine	24, 62
freedoms	2

G

General Rules	23
give way	23, 27, 49
glider	24, 26, 61
go around	49, 50
ground avoidance	34, 39
ground signals	59
ground to air visual code	132

H

heading	65
height	34, 36, 64, 75
helicopter	24, 32
heliport	111
hijack	40
holding bay	94
holding point	94, 97, 106

I

ICAO	1
ice	91
identification beacon	98, 116
IFR	31, 39, 80
IFR in controlled airspace	40
IFR pre-flight requirements	40
illness	16
IMC	65
IMC rating	18, 40
INCERFA	130
incident	121, 123, 125
information signs	107
injury	123, 124, 126
Instrument Flight Rules	31, 39, 71, 74
Instrument Meteorological Conditions	65
interception signals	45
international flight	12, 37

J

JAA	4
JAR	4
Joint Aviation Authority	4

L

landing	25, 45, 49, 59, 60, 72, 88, 92
landing area	63
landing direction indicator	95, 116
landing distance available	88, 114
landing	95
LDA	88, 114
licence	15, 18
licence validity	17
lifejackets	11
liferafts	11
light signals	46
lights	11, 26, 46, 51, 99, 115

M

maintenance	9, 110
manoeuvring area	59, 62, 72, 87
markers	107, 115, 116
marshalling	52
mayday	51, 75
medical certificate	16, 17
meteorological conditions	32, 35, 65
Military Air Traffic Zone	73
minimum altitude	39
modifications	9
movement area	62, 87, 110

N

national licence	17
National PPL	17
night	20, 26, 34, 45, 46, 65, 95
noise certificate	4, 12
NOTAM	1, 16

O

obstacle	34, 39, 108, 115
operator	125
overtaking	24, 26

P

pan	51
PANS	1
PAPI	105
passengers	18, 19, 20
Permit to Fly	9
PPL requirements	17
PPL training	17
pressure altitude	36, 64, 74
Procedures for Air Navigation	1
proficiency check	19
Prohibited Area	70, 77

Q

QFE	36, 64
QNH	36, 64
quadrantal rules	35, 38

R

Radar Service	73
RAS	74
rating	17, 18
rating renewal	19
rating validity	19
Recommended Practices	1, 4
reference code	87
regional QNH	36
registration marks	3
remuneration	17
renewal of rating	19
repairs	10
rescue and fire fighting	110
rescue co-ordination centre	129, 133
responsibilities of pilot	5, 9, 12, 15, 32, 40, 52, 130
restricted airspace	1, 69
Restricted Area	70, 77
revalidation	19
right of way	23, 27
RIS	74
risk of collision	23, 27
Rules of the Air	4, 23, 31
runway	63, 87, 88, 91, 109, 112

runway designator	95
runway lights	98
runway markings	95, 96
runway strip	92, 112
runway surface	89
RVSM	38

S

safety-sensitive personnel	66
SAR	129
Search and Rescue	129
secondary radar	74
semicircular rules	38
separation	72, 74
servicing	110
signal area	94, 116
signal lamp	94
signals from ATC	46
signals from marshaller	52
signals to marshaller	58
signals to surface vessel	131
signs	106
simulated instrument flight	18
slush	91, 115
snow	91, 115
sovereignty	2
Special VFR	35, 71, 74, 80
speed restriction	34
squawk	40, 45, 75
SSR	45, 74
Standard Pressure Setting	36
Standards	1, 4
State of Registry	2, 15, 121, 125
stopway	88, 89, 92, 93, 99, 113
student pilot	16
symbols	132

T

take-off	24, 47, 59, 60, 72, 88, 89, 92
take-off distance available	89, 114
take-off run available	89, 114
taxi	47
taxi-holding position	94, 97, 106, 112
taxiing	59, 63
taxiway	63, 91, 93, 109, 112
taxiway lights	101
taxiway markings	95, 97
threshold	88, 96, 98, 109, 114
TODA	89, 114
TORA	89, 114
touchdown zone	96, 114
towing	24
traffic pattern	61, 72
transition altitude	36, 37, 64
transition layer	36, 37
transition level	36, 37
transponder	40, 45, 74
Type Approval	9

U

uncertainty	130, 133
unlawful interference	40
urgency	51, 75

V

valid licence	17
validation	15
validity of rating	19
vectors	74
VFR	31, 35, 80
VFR minima	32
VFR restrictions	34
visibility	32, 35, 65
visual aids on aerodromes	94
Visual Flight Rules	31, 35, 72
Visual Meteorological Conditions	65
VMC	32, 65

W

water	11, 34, 37, 89, 130
weighing	10
wind direction indicator	95
windsock	95

Notes

Notes

Notes

Notes